Praise for *Walking w*

Going to college is a once-in-a-lifetime opportunity for social and intellectual growth. It should also be a time for spiritual growth—for learning to walk with Jesus. Stephen Kellough has been teaching students how to make that walk for more than twenty-five years as a campus pastor. In this engaging book, Kellough uses his skill as a storyteller and experience as a shepherd of the human soul to address exactly the issues that college students face today.

PHILIP RYKEN *President, Wheaton College*

This is an enormously helpful book that should be in the hands of every Christian student on a college campus. It is filled with wisdom coming from a chaplain whose long experience with campus ministry was extensive, celebrated, and filled with good judgment. This is a book to recommend to students who are struggling and everyone who is supporting them through their college years.

GARY M. BURGE *Professor of New Testament, Calvin Theological Seminary*

Steve Kellough has spent his life loving, serving, and strengthening college students. This book overflows with wisdom and grace on every page. If you or your child is stepping into the world of higher education, then this is a must-read.

MARGARET FEINBERG *Author of* Taste and See: Discovering God among Butchers, Bakers, and Fresh Food Makers

With years of experience in listening to and mentoring students, Stephen Kellough has written a thoughtful and insightful book on the challenges Christian students face today. *Walking with Jesus on Campus* is an important, practical guide for both students and those walking with them in their spiritual journey. Highly recommended.

DENNIS P. HOLLINGER *President and Professor of Christian Ethics, Gordon-Conwell Theological Seminary*

Unfortunately, for college students who desire to follow Jesus, the journey through university education is a test of faith that many do not pass. But for those who would read this book and put into practice what Steve teaches, they will not only survive their college years but find that they will thrive during this formative season of spiritual growth.

TOM YEAKLEY *The Navigators, Collegiate Staff Equipper, former US Collegiate Ministry Director*

What I would do if I could have had a wiser mentor to help me navigate my formative college years. I am so thankful for Chaplain Kellough, a humble sage who gives us just that. This book gives us a window into the countless years of wisdom gleaned from his faithful ministry to generations of students in some of their most difficult years. And through it all, he reminds us where our hope is, in a God of grace and love.

DAVID CHOI *Lead Pastor of Church of the Beloved, Chicago*

In *Walking with Jesus on Campus*, Stephen Kellough provides a wonderful, spiritual road map for college students. Stephen's wisdom from his ministry as a college chaplain provide a depth of insight into the spiritual development of college students. I recommend this book to every college student, counselor, chaplain, faculty, and mentor. This will be a valuable resource for years to come.

VALENCIA WIGGINS *Psychologist, educator, and speaker*

I listen to everything Stephen Kellough says. He has lived the life of a peripatetic pastor. He walked this campus. Here, he walked with Jesus, and he walked with our people. After decades of faithful and wise pastoral leadership, Kellough shows us how to care for your soul during college. If you are a college student or work with one, *Walking with Jesus on Campus* might just be the most important book you read.

TIM BLACKMON *Chaplain, Wheaton College*

Steve Kellough knows what he is talking about! As a chaplain and spiritual guide for twenty-five years at Wheaton College, he is well familiar with the issues and concerns of college students. In this volume, Steve provides godly wisdom on timely topics using real-life examples and pertinent reflection questions. While at Wheaton, the students affectionately called him "Chappy K" because they had real respect for him, felt comfortable in his presence, and trusted him as a mentor. So pull up a chair, and sit under "Chappy K's" counsel—for the first time or once again. You will be consoled, encouraged, and challenged in your journey as an apprentice of Jesus.

EDEE SCHULZE *Vice President for Student Life, Westmont College*

Steve Kellough's *Walking with Jesus on Campus* is the book every Christian college student needs. Its wise, practical, thoroughly biblical counsel is the product of its author's well-honed pastoral gifts and his years of experience in shepherding students. I witnessed that ministry closely during our seventeen years of working together on a single campus; I can testify to its effectiveness. Thus it delights me to think that now, through this very readable book, future generations of Christian students everywhere will be able to come under Chaplain Steve's gracious pastoral care.

DUANE LITFIN *President Emeritus, Wheaton College*

Steve Kellough brought to the Wheaton chaplaincy wisdom, clarity, and the quiet skills of a good shepherd. All of this and more is reflected in this wonderful guide for the college student who wants to navigate through the college journey as a Christian. He touches on the issues that most resonate with the concerns and questions that students have and experience. The result is not the typical book of platitudes or abstract ideas, but down-to-earth advice that is both profound and realistic in its expectations.

DENNIS OKHOLM *Professor of Theology, Azusa Pacific University*

The stressful rigors of academic routines and the rapid pace of campus life often threaten to eclipse the important disciplines that enable a student's soul to flourish. Graduates may be intellectually and professionally prepared yet shallow and sometimes languishing at the center of their being. My friend Stephen Kellough has spent years sharing with students the principles that lead to a flourishing life with Jesus at the center. And now, thankfully, he has shared this treasure with all of us in a particularly noteworthy book. The call of this book reminds me of the wisdom of the writer of Proverbs, "Above all else, guard your heart, for everything you do flows from it" (Proverbs 4:23). I can't think of a better gift to give graduating high school students or students in the throes of college life!

JOE STOWELL *President, Cornerstone University, Grand Rapids, MI*

This book should be required reading for every Christian student during their college or university years. Drawing on a lifetime of pastoral experience and offering a deeply biblical understanding of spiritual formation, Stephen Kellough speaks to the hearts of God's people with a clear, wise voice.

JEFFREY GREENMAN *President, Regent College, Vancouver, BC*

Walking with Jesus on Campus by Stephen Kellough is a well-written, concise, and very helpful book on how to care for one's soul during college, but it will also be a real blessing to readers beyond the college years. It covers ten key topics: embracing the love of God, weakness, perfectionism, doubt and depression, the Sabbath as a gift, sexuality and singleness, servanthood, community, revival, and being apprenticed to Jesus. Highly recommended!

SIANG-YANG TAN *Professor of Psychology, Fuller Theological Seminary; Senior Pastor of First Evangelical Church Glendale; author of* Counseling and Psychotherapy: A Christian Perspective and Shepherding God's People

Stephen Kellough draws upon his twenty-five years of counseling students at Wheaton College to provide a helpful guide for Christian students who may struggle with the challenges of the college experience. He shows that issues such as doubt and depression are not uncommon and points to relevant Scriptures and sage advice from Christian authors to enable students to walk joyfully with Jesus.

EDWIN M. YAMAUCHI *Professor of History Emeritus, Miami University, OH*

I wish I had this book available to me when I was in college. I remember asking and dealing with many of these questions that Chaplain Kellough carefully addresses. Even now, I found myself greatly benefited by reading *Walking with Jesus on Campus*.

GENE FROST *Executive Director, Wheaton Academy Foundation*

Statistics seem to indicate that more and more collegians are walking away from the faith of their youth. Is there hope in this troubling trend? After years as a pastor and a quarter century as a college chaplain, Stephen Kellough offers insightful experience and sage advice on the care of souls. College students, as well as their parents and mentors, will find vital help in navigating the challenges of walking with Christ, rather than away from him, during the college years.

DONNA THOENNES *Biola University*

There is much wisdom here borne out of the experience of "walking" with generations of college students. The brilliance of Chaplain Kellough's "walking" is that he does so not behind or in front of students, but beside them. We simply need more good "walkers" like Chaplain Kellough on college campuses.

JOSEPH B. MODICA *University Chaplain, Eastern University*

I wish I had this book in hand before I went to college. Brimming with wisdom and practical insights, this important and beautiful work reveals what is most essential in our lives. It will help a student, or anyone at any age, make more than a living—it will inspire them to build a life.

KEN SHIGEMATSU *Pastor of Tenth Church, Vancouver, BC, and bestselling author of* Survival Guide for the Soul

Walking with Jesus on Campus is a treasure of life-giving wisdom for students of all ages. As a frequent Wheaton chapel speaker, I saw the love between students and Chaplain Steve Kellough—the same love that inspires this beautiful book revealing how biblical truth is the highest love for human beings. I recommend it highly!

KELLY MONROE KULLBERG *Founder, the Veritas Forum; author,* Finding God beyond Harvard: The Quest for Veritas*; founder, American Association of Evangelicals (AAE)*

WALKING

WITH

JESUS

ON CAMPUS

How to Care for Your Soul during College

STEPHEN
KELLOUGH

MOODY PUBLISHERS
CHICAGO

Names and details of some stories have been changed to protect the privacy of individuals.

Edited by Michelle Sincock
Interior and Cover Design: Erik M. Peterson
Cover illustration of path graphic copyright © 2018 by кирилл поляшенко / iStock (1063174100). All rights reserved.
Cover photo of building copyright © 2018 by ChrisBellPhoto / iStock (149103). All rights reserved.
Author photo: Mike Hudson Photography

ISBN: 978-0-8024-1926-2

To my wife, Linda, and our son, Jeffrey—
with thanksgiving to God
for your spiritual insights, your encouraging words,
and your walk with Jesus.

Table of Contents

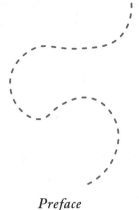

Preface

A Book for College (and Beyond)

I'm writing this book from my perspective after completing a full career as a college chaplain. What is a college chaplain? The military, hospitals, and prisons have chaplains, but colleges? Simply put, a college chaplain is a campus pastor.

Pastoral ministry on campus covers spiritual counseling and mentoring of students—formal and informal—during office hours, in lecture halls, at the gym, and on the sidewalk. The chaplain's role is being pastorally present with students.

The chaplain's work happens in unscripted conversations as well as prepared worship services. My chaplaincy experience has been in the context of a confessional Christian institution with a chapel attendance requirement, and my oversight of chapel has provided an opportunity to impact campus culture and encourage faith in the lives of students.

In this book, I'm addressing ten Achilles' heel issues that concern students most, and I'm sharing some of what I have learned from students themselves about the life of the spirit and the life of the mind. Thus, my primary audience is those currently experiencing (or about to experience) college or university life.

My goal is to help the Christian student set spiritual priorities—not just to *survive* the college experience but to *thrive* as a follower of Christ. However, I have a secondary audience in mind as well. The issues explored here impact adult readers beyond college who seek to live in a godly way in a challenging world.

As I have witnessed students grappling with matters that bear on their life of faith, I have been challenged myself by the Scriptures, church history, culture, antagonists, colleagues, and student friends. In this volume, I am drawing from resources that can make a difference in bringing help, hope, and healing to our faith walk.

In writing this book, I imagine myself with a student seeking answers sitting in my office or maybe over a hot beverage in a coffee shop. I invite you to join me in thinking seriously about walking in the way that Jesus would have us walk.

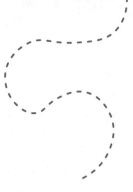

Introduction

A Spiritual Walk

The phone rang, and I immediately recognized the faculty member's voice. But this time her tone was soft, and her words were unusually hesitant. A distraught student was in her office, and she asked if it would be okay for this struggling freshman to meet with me. We scheduled a time, and the student arrived as planned.

Jacob had made a successful transition to campus life during the early months of the fall semester. He enjoyed his classes and new friendships through dorm life and club activities. But now, his life was a blur.

Late the previous evening, Jacob received word from home that his good friend Matthew had died. Matthew, one of Jacob's closest friends, was attending a community college back home. His death was shocking as he suddenly collapsed during an intramural soccer game. This was Jacob's first experience with the death of someone he knew so well.

During my initial meeting with Jacob, his tears flowed easily, and his words came with difficulty. Jacob's emotions were raw. Long stretches of silence were not unproductive, however, as we struggled together in grieving and in longing for divine help.

My first meeting with Jacob was not my last. Formally and informally we caught up with each other over the course of the year. Thankfully, Jacob found additional help and encouragement through friends, faculty, and the counseling center.

My heart goes out to college students who sincerely seek the face of God in the midst of their pain and trouble through prayer, the Bible, and Christian community. For twenty-five years I walked the college campus. It's a joy to recognize a student's face and to stop for brief conversation, sometimes taking a quick moment to pray for a pressing concern.

But my "walking" as chaplain was more than a trip from place to place. A key dimension of my job consisted of walking with students spiritually. As a "brother in the Lord" to younger apprentices in Christ, I had the privilege of sharing faith lessons with anyone eager to learn. It was my great delight to join in the journey with fellow Christ followers—walking together.

THE WALKING METAPHOR

"Walking" is a biblical word.[1] Throughout the Scriptures, we find hundreds of references to the act of "walking." Early in the Bible, in Genesis 3:8, we read of God "walking in the garden in the cool of the day."

But "walking," in a figurative sense, means "living." In

the Old and New Testaments we find this metaphorical use of "walking" as "living in a certain way." In Genesis 5:22 and 24, we read about Enoch, who is commended with the phrase, "Enoch walked faithfully with God." Psalm 1:1 says, "Blessed is the one who does not walk in step with the wicked." We find in the familiar text of Micah 6:8, "And what does the LORD require of you? To act justly and to love mercy and to walk humbly with your God." In the New Testament, in John 8:12, Jesus says, "I am the light of the world. Whoever follows me will never walk in darkness, but will have the light of life."

In many of the apostle Paul's letters, we find the word *peripateo* translated as "walk" in some versions and "live" in other versions, such as in Galatians 5:16: "So I say, walk [or live] by the Spirit and you will not gratify the desires of the flesh."

Living the Christian life—walking the path, following Jesus—can be complicated and difficult. Even with an abundance of spiritual resources, we stumble over potholes in the road because of our sinful nature. In the midst of this internal struggle, how do we cope? How do we stay on the right path? In the apostle's words, "So I say, walk [or live] by the Spirit" (Gal. 5:16).

Thankfully, this war of opposite forces—the sinful nature versus the Holy Spirit—is not a war of equal forces. The Holy Spirit is not a limited resource. As followers of Jesus, we are people who actually can live by the divine power of the Spirit who dwells within us as our guide and enabler.

With the Holy Spirit, we have walking power. There is a shoe company called Easy Spirit. They sell only women's shoes—my wife has a pair. Easy Spirit. I like that. It sounds biblical. It ties in with what Jesus said, "My yoke is easy, and my burden is light" (Matt. 11:30).

Can you see how this view of the spiritual life opens us up to freedom and liberty? Instead of looking at the Christian life as a burden or a duty to try harder and work more feverishly to gain God's approval, we're commanded and encouraged to "walk by the Spirit" (Gal. 5:16).

But how does this work? Is God just a genie at our beck and call? This is not a matter of hocus-pocus. Our walk by the Spirit begins and continues through prayer. By faith, we place our confidence in Christ and leave it to Him to lead us. By His Word and in a moment by moment trust relationship, God will show us the way. When we walk by the Spirit our burdens are lighter because we are going God's way and not our own way.

A spiritual mentor of mine, Dr. J. Richard Chase, was an articulate communicator. His prayers were always sensitive and thoughtful, and for some reason, I noticed a phrase that Dr. Chase commonly repeated in his prayers. He would pray, regularly and fervently, that God would "guide and direct." I cannot think of two more appropriate words to be included in our petitions to God in prayer, that God by His Holy Spirit would guide us and direct us on the path we should walk.

In Jesus' day, "walking" was the primary means of transportation. Middle Easterners in the first century were not living in the age of planes, trains, and automobiles. And even though walking is a slow method of travel, the idea of "walking" includes the sense of making progress.

Therefore, when we speak of "walking in the Spirit" as a means of spiritual formation, we are speaking of making progress in our spiritual life.[2] Walking may be slow, but we are going somewhere. And when we are walking by the Spirit, we are traveling on the right road and making progress in the right direction.

Dallas Willard provides this definition: "Spiritual formation for the Christian basically refers to the Spirit-driven process of forming the inner world of the human self in such a way that it becomes like the inner being of Christ himself."[3] It is my prayer that as we proceed chapter by chapter, our "inner world" will grow in that "Spirit-driven process" of becoming more and more like Jesus.

BABY STEPS

One of my favorite movies is a Bill Murray film that came out in 1991. In *What about Bob?*, Bob Wiley (Murray), a troubled man who is afraid of everything, seeks professional help from his new therapist, Dr. Leo Marvin (Richard Dreyfuss).

Dr. Marvin is a bestselling author, and he provides Bob with a copy of his new book, *Baby Steps*, as a resource. The secret to Dr. Marvin's therapeutic approach involved counseling his patients to take "baby steps" in achieving recovery and healing.

Even as I consider my own pastoral counsel to students and others who are struggling with difficult issues in their own walks, I sometimes think of this book title and the principle of baby steps. Taking small, deliberate, thoughtful, careful steps makes good sense. So let's begin the walk.

God does not love us
because we are good;
God loves us because
God is good.

Chapter One

The Most Significant Spiritual Challenge in College

About five or six years into my chaplaincy, I experienced an eye-opening, "aha" moment. Suddenly, it all became clear. I could now answer the question that I had heard time and again, "What is the most significant spiritual challenge for college students?"

Here's how it happened. It was lunchtime in the college dining commons where I was hosting a meal with an off-campus guest. Eight or nine of us circled the large round table in the faculty dining room. A few faculty and a few students joined our guest and myself. As an incurable optimist, I always expect the most out of these informal gatherings. Often, I am disappointed. On this day, I was not.

Our guest was posing deep and probing questions, and the conversation proved to be enjoyable and enlightening. Then came the clincher: "What have you found to be the most significant spiritual challenge facing today's college student?" she asked. Silence. We all realized the importance of this inquiry, and no one was willing to break in with a half-baked response.

It was a familiar question, but it needed a substantive answer. With contributions from several around the table, here's the answer we settled on: "The most significant spiritual challenge facing today's college student is to know that they are loved by God." We all agreed.

It doesn't sound very deep, doesn't have the ring of profundity. But I have been convinced over and over that this is indeed the supreme struggle for undergraduate students. And it's probably the same for graduate students, faculty, staff, and anyone else of any age who is thoughtful, sincere, and spiritually sensitive. However, in my pastoral experience, I have found that undergrad college students are often the quickest to agree with that assessment and to eagerly seek a remedy for their personal lives.

EMBRACING THE LOVE OF GOD

One of my colleagues in ministry, another college chaplain, James Bryan Smith of Friends University, has articulated this spiritual hunger that is so common and critical in the lives of students. His book *Embracing the Love of God* has received widespread circulation, and I have given away his book more times than I can remember.

Here's how Chaplain Jim begins telling his own story and his personal struggle with knowing and experiencing the love of God:

I lived my early Christian life with the belief that God really did not like me. God tolerated me, I thought, in the hopes of improving me. One day I just might get myself together, quit sinning, and start behaving like Jesus. Then, I was certain, God would approve of me.

I got up early almost every day, praying and reading the Bible between five and seven in the morning. I fasted once a week, spent time helping the poor, and maintained straight A's in all of my classes. I entertained the idea of becoming a monk because I figured that by abandoning the pleasures of this world I would please God even more.

In a slow, almost imperceptible way, I developed an unhealthy conception of God. As a result, the Christian life became a painful drudgery. On the outside I appeared joyful and upbeat, but beneath the holy veneer lurked a bitter and unhappy person who secretly hated himself and the god he served.[1] [His use of the lower case letter "g" is intentional.]

What a story. That's where James Bryan Smith found himself in his own spiritual journey before arriving at an awareness of this biblical truth: God does not love us because we are good; God loves us because God is good.

This is the testimony of a sincere Christian who struggled to know God and to serve God. But it's the sad testimony of an unhappy and confused existence based on a faulty view of God. It's an all too common view that fails to understand the truth, the beauty, and the depth of the love of God.

Addressing the topic of the love of God does not require anything stunningly unique. Here, my interest is simple and straightforward in offering a reminder of something we already know. It's my prayer that we might all be encouraged to embrace the biblical truth of the love of God in such a way that we would not simply *know* it, but we would *experience* it.

A BIBLICAL FOUNDATION

One of the most important and helpful texts on this topic is from the first epistle of the apostle John. Our text is 1 John 4:14–19:

> And we have seen and testify that the Father has sent his Son to be the Savior of the world. If anyone acknowledges that Jesus is the Son of God, God lives in them and they in God. And so we know and rely on the love God has for us.
>
> God is love. Whoever lives in love lives in God, and God in them. This is how love is made complete among us so that we will have confidence on the day of judgment: In this world we are like Jesus. There is no fear in love. But perfect love drives out fear, because fear has to do with punishment. The one who fears is not made perfect in love.
>
> We love because he first loved us.

We need this passage of Scripture. We need to take it as prescriptive medicine for our sick souls. A psychiatrist once reported this statement coming from a sincere but desperate patient: "Make me sure that there is a God of love and I shall go away a well man."[2] Late in the first century, the apostle John wrote his letter to Christian churches in Asia Minor. It was a letter written to Christian men and women who desperately needed the reminder that the God they worshiped and served was a God of love.

John's purpose in 1 John 4 is to motivate his Christian friends to be people of love. And his argument in these six verses is that because God is love, because God has loved us in Christ, and because God continues to love us—we, therefore, must be people who love each other. It's a very practical message based on a very profound theological concept.

The love of God is such a deep and dynamic concept that it eludes a simple definition. God's love is, of course, more than emotion. It is a combination of qualities involving devotion, loyalty, kindness, grace, and mercy. A. W. Tozer's book, *The Knowledge of the Holy*, is one of the most helpful volumes on the attributes of God. But Tozer professes ignorance in proposing a comprehensive definition of God's love. Tozer writes:

> If we would know God and for others' sakes tell what we know, we must try to speak of His love. All Christians have tried, but none has ever done it very well. I can no more do justice to that awesome and wonder-filled theme than a child can grasp a star. Still, by reaching toward the star the child may call attention to it and even indicate the direction one must look to see it. . . .
>
> We do not know, and we may never know, what love *is*, but we can know how it manifests itself.[3]

So how can we even begin to grasp the meaning of God's love? We have to point here and there in Scripture to various descriptions of the "love of God." We'll never understand God's love completely. But we can grow step by step in our appreciation for that quality of the divine life and love of Jesus, who is the reason for our creation, our redemption, and our eternal life.

PERFECT LOVE DRIVES OUT FEAR

The arrow that I would like to shoot at the text of 1 John chapter 4 lands in the middle of verse 16–17. "God is love. Whoever lives in love lives in God, and God in them. This is how love is made complete among us so that we will have confidence on the day of judgment: In this world we are like Jesus."

When we think of the perfection of God's love, we see it in His very character. God is perfect (Heb. 7:26) and God is love (1 John 4:8)—therefore God's love is perfect. With God's love there are no flaws, no mistakes, no limitations. Absolutely perfect.

But hold on. There's an additional way of thinking of the perfect love of God, and we see it here in 1 John 4. Dallas Willard calls it, "the four movements toward perfect love."[4] In 1 John 4:19 we read, "He first loved us." This is where love begins. Its source is God. The second movement of perfect love comes as we reciprocate God's love for us and we fulfill the greatest commandment in loving God. "We love because he first loved us" (1 John 4:19).

Movements three and four are next as believers love "one another"—in the words of 1 John 4:12, "If we love one another, God lives in us and his love is made complete in us." These are the four movements of perfect love: God loves us; we love God; we love others; others love us.

Therefore, in this sequence of four movements we see

how love is "made complete among us" (1 John 4:17). This "completed love," this "perfect love," is not just God's love for us or our love for God or our love for others or others' love for us—it's all of the above. And when we receive and extend these dimensions of the love of God, in the words of the apostle, "We will have confidence on the day of judgment: In this world we are like Jesus" (v. 17).

The children of God and the Son of God are loved by the Father. As God's children, we can face the trials and temptations of life with confidence because we have the Father's love to see us through. Life altogether changes for us when we understand and embrace the truth that God loves us.

This is why the apostle can go on to say, "There is no fear in love" (v. 18). In our English language we have incorporated use of the word phobia coming from the Greek word *phobos*. I don't know if you have a phobia. There are all kinds of phobias—acrophobia, claustrophobia, and so on. I asked my wife what the fear of snakes is called. She said, "It's called normal."

In our text, 1 John 4:17–18, the apostle John is speaking about the fear of judgment. Technically, that would be called *krisisphobia*.[5] In the final judgment, eternal life awaits those who are trusting Christ while eternal punishment is the future for those who have rejected Christ (John 3:36). Therefore, our response to Jesus makes all the difference in the world—for now, and for eternity. When we embrace the Savior, we not only inherit an abundant future in the presence of God, but we receive the Holy Spirit whose perfect love within us drives out fear.

Let me tell you about a woman who grew up in a home that had an alarming absence of love.[6] She lived almost her whole childhood in an atmosphere without love or forgiveness. Whenever her parents discovered a mistake she made, she was punished. And her condemning parents made sure she understood that her mistakes were sins.

As this young women moved into adulthood, she couldn't forget anything that she had done wrong. She remembered it all, and she felt guilty about it all. Fortunately, she found a Christian counselor who helped her receive and appreciate God's forgiveness. As she experienced spiritual healing, she felt like a new person with a new beginning. She felt like a child again, being welcomed into the arms of Jesus.

This woman knew the hurt that comes with the fear of judgment. You might say that her fear was a fear of God's ultimate judgment, but all of that changed dramatically when she received God's forgiveness, acceptance, and healing. She became a witness to the truth that God's perfect love drives out fear.

TRUE GUILT AND FALSE GUILT

As we consider the matter of fearing the judgment of God, it is important to recognize a distinction between true guilt and false guilt. I suspect that, for the woman whose story I just told, there was some true guilt and there was some false guilt, but she needed help in separating one from the other. The person with true guilt feels guilty because the guilt has been earned by sinning against God. With true guilt, the solution comes with confession, repentance, forgiveness, and possibly even restoration. When we come to God with a repentant heart, God is always willing to forgive and to remove the guilt of our sins. The psalmist describes his experience this way:

> Then I acknowledged my sin to you
>> and did not cover up my iniquity.
> I said, "I will confess
>> my transgressions to the LORD."
> And you forgave
>> the guilt of my sin. (Ps. 32:5)

Pastor and theologian John Stott helps us understand the meaning of repentance by saying first that it is more than shame or remorse. Instead, it is turning away from what has displeased God and turning in the direction of what pleases God.[7] This means that repentance involves a constant determination to "turn from sin" and "turn to Christ." It's a commitment to follow Jesus.

But what if our feelings of guilt remain even after our confession and repentance? Indeed, that is what often plagues the most sincere believers. We acknowledge our sin and we receive God's forgiveness, but we fail to remember that God has *really* forgiven us. We have been forgiven. We do not stand guilty before God. But we feel guilty. I believe that part of this is quite natural, and we might even expect it. There are consequences to sin. We reap what we sow. And it may take time to heal a guilty conscience. But with forgiveness there is healing, and we should also expect healing.

Dr. Earl Wilson, in his book *Counseling and Guilt*, suggests that it is helpful to remind people who struggle in this way: "You may still feel bad about your sin but you need to know that God is not stuck on it. God has more important things to think about. Christ died so that sin could be forgiven and right living restored."[8] That's pretty direct. But sometimes that's what we need to hear. When we find ourselves suffering with unresolved guilt, it is often because we have too high a view of sin, and too low a view of God.[9] The words of 1 John 4:9–10 are a good reminder:

> This is how God showed his love among us: He sent his one and only Son into the world that we might live through him. This is love: not that we loved God, but that he loved us and sent his Son as an atoning sacrifice for our sins.

Jesus sacrificed Himself in our place, and we need to accept His true forgiveness—which is easier said than done. True forgiveness that comes through the cross of Christ is absolute forgiveness. Once we have confessed our sin and determined to turn from that sin in sincere repentance, we are forgiven. And then, we need to embrace that forgiveness. We need to believe that God can and does forgive. It is the height of arrogance for us on this side of forgiveness to claim that more needs to be done.

Studying biblical texts on guilt and forgiveness or meditating on familiar passages like Psalm 103:12 or 1 John 1:9 may help. Conversation with a trusted Christian friend can be encouraging. When guilt is overwhelming, an experienced pastor or counselor may be beneficial. With our prayers, God uses various means of delivering hope.

In the chaplain's office, I have welcomed student after student who has been burdened with guilt and shame. Sometimes the guilt and shame are linked to personal sin, and there is personal responsibility associated with the removal of that pain. But the removal of pain is not the ultimate goal. It is godly sorrow, repentance, and acceptance of God's forgiveness that leads to a healing that lifts guilt and pain.

I remember Ryan, whose academic struggles were complicated by physical symptoms, including an inability to sleep. College work was too demanding for Ryan during his first semester, even though his high school grades and his college entrance exams were stellar. Once Ryan became convinced of the safety of revealing more to me, he was able to disclose details of a dating relationship that had gone too far physically. Through a slow and gentle process, Ryan confessed and repented of his sin, embraced God's true forgiveness, and found relief of the true guilt he had been carrying. As Ryan grew in his understanding of the unconditional love of God, he came to appreciate the ultimate source of a dramatic healing. It was God who restored his spiritual health, mental health, and even physical health.

So in the case of true guilt, the solution is true forgiveness. In the case of false guilt, or unearned guilt, the situation is quite different. In counseling other students, I have observed how guilt can be traced to overwhelming demands and unrealistic expectations of a campus culture or a home life. In those cases, it comes as a relief to identify one's guilt as false guilt that can be and must be eliminated by embracing the love of God that drives out fear.

Unearned guilt feelings come in great quantities among high achievers, perfectionists, and Christian students. The suffering of false guilt is just as painful as the suffering associated with true guilt. The self-condemnation of unearned guilt is usually revealed in statements about what a person thinks they "should have" done.[10] "I should have done better." "I should have studied longer." "I should have been more careful." "I shouldn't have let down my parents." These guilt feelings may come completely from within, or they may have their source in the unrealistic expectations imposed by others.

So what is the solution to unearned guilt? The solution is not forgiveness, because forgiveness is not required. The solution to unearned guilt comes in understanding the love of God that casts out these fears.

This may be the time to consider another sense of "the fear of God." The book of Proverbs describes the fear of the Lord as "the beginning of knowledge" (1:7) and "the beginning of wisdom" (9:10). Fearing God in this positive sense means revering Him so much that we desire to please Him alone. With that as our aim, we become less inclined to fear people, and we become less impacted by false guilt.

Guilt and shame and fear can paralyze us. These things can immobilize us. They can stall us. But we have no inadequacy that will separate us from the love of Christ once we are His children. In the words of the apostle Paul, "I am convinced that neither death nor life, neither angels nor demons, neither the present nor the future, nor any powers, neither height nor depth, **nor anything else** in all creation, will be able to separate us from the love of God that is in Christ Jesus our Lord" (Rom. 8:38–39).

LOOK AT THE BIRDS

Jerry Kirk is a pastor friend from Cincinnati who I invited to campus to speak to students.[11] In one of his talks, Jerry told us how as a teenager he suffered with all kinds of inferiority feelings. He came to faith in Christ at the age of eighteen, but because his "receiving mechanism" was all messed-up, as he describes it, he couldn't comprehend that God loved him.

Even so, Jerry attended college and seminary, was ordained as a pastor, and went on to lead a large and influential church. Yet, even as a successful pastor, Jerry felt it was extremely difficult for him to believe that God loved him. Oh, he knew it with his head, but he didn't know it with his heart. Instead, he always felt inadequate, that he never measured up, that his life and work were performance oriented.

Jerry went on to explain that one day, a member of his congregation shared something with him. Of course, she didn't know what her pastor was struggling with. The woman told Jerry how she had been regularly experiencing the affirmation of the love of God. She had a special way of reminding herself of God's love. It was a formula of sorts, a trigger mechanism. Every time she saw a cardinal, she was reminded of the love of God. She would stop to say, "Doris, I love you"—as if those words were coming directly from God.

Jerry liked this idea, so he started searching for cardinals himself. Every time he would see one, he stopped and said (as if repeating the words from God), "Jerry, I love you." And he would start talking to God.

But this wasn't enough for Jerry Kirk. After looking only for cardinals, Jerry decided to extend his search to birds of any kind. And as far as I know, to this day, Jerry is still looking for birds and finding God's regular reminder, "Jerry, I love you."

I don't know what kind of reminder you need, but if you are like me, you need one. You might try the bird thing. When you read the Scriptures, see how clear the message is that God loves you. Our text reminds us, "God is love. This is how God showed his love among us: He sent his one and only Son into the world that we might live through him" (1 John 4:8b–9).

You might want to start each day with a prayer like this: Loving God, help me to know, believe, and experience Your deep, deep love for me.

A Step Further

- *What is the most significant spiritual challenge for you right now?*

- *Do you believe the Creator of all things actually loves you?*

- *Do you "feel" loved by God even if you "know" you are loved?*

- *Do you find yourself growing in your love for God?*

- *Do you feel a sense of burden to "please" God or be a "better" person in order for Him to love you more?*

- *What's the difference between fearing God and fearing God's judgment?*

- *Are you feeling true/false guilt? In what ways?*

- *What is the appropriate approach to each of these types of guilt?*

The greater our human weakness,
the more noticeable the
grace and the power of God.

Chapter Two

Weakness—Not Such a Bad Thing

The week before final exams, the busyness of the chaplain's office significantly reduces. Students hunker down in the library, in dorm rooms, or wherever a quiet space can be found to complete term papers and study for exams.

When Andrew stepped into my office on one particular afternoon, he had a worried look and a frightened demeanor. As he sat across from me in a comfortable office chair, I tried to put him at ease with some friendly, welcoming words. That lasted only briefly as Andrew got to the point of his visit.

Andrew explained that he didn't know if he would make it through final exams. High school had been a breeze, but college was altogether different. The potential for lower grades loomed over his courses. How could he face his parents with grades falling short? What would he do with his ambition of medical school, if that had to be set aside?

Andrew's experience is not unusual for first-year college students. He was discovering that the world of higher education is populated by a ton of smart people. Immersion into such an intellectual environment reveals weakness, and this is what Andrew was feeling. His inability to achieve perfect grades demonstrated a universal characteristic of human beings—in body and mind we are all weak and needy.

2 CORINTHIANS 12:7–10—PUTTING WEAKNESS INTO PERSPECTIVE

There's a text of Scripture that can help us put our weakness into perspective: 2 Corinthians 12:7–10. It's a familiar text that comes from the life and ministry of the apostle Paul. In his second letter to the Corinthians, Paul's primary purpose is to defend his apostleship. Proud false teachers had infiltrated the church at Corinth, and Paul responds to them.

In the opening verses of chapter 12, Paul speaks of the visions and revelations that he had received personally and directly from the Lord. But beginning in verse seven, the apostle puts it all into perspective:

> **To keep me from becoming conceited, I was given a thorn in my flesh, a messenger of Satan, to torment me. Three times I pleaded with the Lord to take it away from me. But he said to me, "My grace is sufficient for you, for my power is made perfect in weakness." Therefore I will boast all the more gladly about my weaknesses, so that Christ's power may rest on me. That is why, for Christ's sake, I delight in weaknesses, in insults, in hardships, in persecutions, in difficulties. For when I am weak, then I am strong.** (2 Cor. 12:7–10)

Paul describes his particular weakness as a "thorn in my flesh." This "thorn" is not specifically identified, and it's humorous to read of the countless speculations that scholars have offered. Many have supposed that it was a physical ailment (and it may well have been). All kinds of illnesses and disabilities have been suggested, including a speech difficulty, malaria, leprosy—or what I find most curious—a dental infection.

Quite commonly, it is thought that Paul might be referring to failing eyesight. Others have thought the thorn might be a spiritual or psychological struggle with doubt, depression, sexual temptation, or guilt from persecuting Christians in the past. Still others have identified Paul's thorn as the opposition he faced by false teachers.[1]

So, in the final analysis, it's probably best that we don't know what the "thorn" was. If we did, we may not apply this text to our own lives and wonder what God might be using as a thorn in the flesh for us. Whatever Paul struggled with, it served the purpose of keeping him humble, and that was the point. It kept the apostle on his knees in prayer. It kept him from boasting in the wrong way.

The apostle Paul identified a thorn in the flesh that revealed his own weakness. It humbled him. It kept him honest. The Greek word for "thorn" is *skolops* and it means "splinter" or "stake." This word *skolops* was used to describe the stakes that the Romans would drive into the ground— stakes upon which criminals would be impaled.[2] This was no minor annoyance.

And it was God who was using this thorn for Paul's sake. Yes, the text does say that the thorn was a "messenger of Satan," but the text also says, "There was given me a thorn in my flesh." That implies "given by God." Very clearly, the thorn had a divine purpose, and Paul appealed to the Lord to remove this hurtful intruder. It was a hindrance, a weakness, and Paul didn't want it.

Before my college chaplaincy, I served for a number of years in church ministry. In my first church, there was a man who was a leader in the congregation who was less than enthusiastic about my being called as pastor. Early in my tenure, this man introduced himself to me saying, "I am going to be your thorn in the flesh." I don't recall my response. Maybe it was something like, "Well, thanks for the warning." Only later did I think that I could have gently reminded him that Paul's thorn in the flesh was a "messenger of Satan." Maybe it's good I didn't.

Paul never did concede that his thorn in the flesh was something "good." It wasn't "good." It was a "messenger of Satan." But it did become an opportunity for the demonstration of the grace of God. The thorn revealed human weakness. The thorn caught Paul's attention. It was painful and it was humiliating, but it accomplished what God intended. The thorn reminded Paul of just how weak and needy he really was. And we are all that way, aren't we? We are weak, and we are needy.

We need the help of 2 Corinthians 12. When we consider the apostle's struggle, we are encouraged and helped in owning up to our own weakness and brokenness. Only then can we begin to appreciate God's purposes and the divine resources available to put it all into perspective.

GOOD NEWS: ALL PEOPLE ARE WEAK

When I was a college student, one of the highly respected authors of the time was Paul Tournier—a Swiss Christian physician whose books reflected well on psychological and spiritual insights. In one of his books, *The Strong and the Weak*, Dr. Tournier claims that all people have "an identical inner personality" in the sense that all people are weak. He writes: "The truth is that human beings are much more alike than they think. What is different is the external mask . . . strong or weak. These appearances, however, hide an identical inner personality. . . . All [people], in fact, are weak."[3]

The biblical view of our humanity is that we are all weak. Earlier in 2 Corinthians 4, Paul uses an illustration from the ancient world, emphasizing our human frailty with the picture of "jars of clay." In that culture, clay pots were used to preserve and protect all kinds of things. People would store their valuables—silver, or gold or other treasures—in clay jars. Paul illustrates how the power of the gospel is entrusted to weak and fragile human vessels. Consistently, throughout Paul's second letter to the Corinthians, there is an emphasis on weakness—our human weakness, our flawed humanity. We are weak. We are frail. We crack. We break.

It's encouraging for us to know that Jesus was also human. He wasn't only human, He was the God-Man, 100% God and 100% man (don't expect me to explain that here). But in Jesus' humanity, He experienced human weakness. The writer to the Hebrews puts it this way: "For we do not have a high priest who is unable to empathize with our weaknesses, but we have one who has been tempted in every way, just as we are—yet he did not sin" (Heb. 4:15).

So even Jesus got tired and got hungry, and he needed rest and food. He ran out of energy and needed to be refreshed, just like we do. Although we are incapable of fully comprehending exactly how the sinless Christ can truly experience human weakness, we must trust the Scriptures that it's true. Jesus struggled in ways that we struggle—even with temptation. That, indeed, is a huge encouragement.

How are you struggling today? Is it physically or intellectually or socially? Are you aware of your struggles? Can you admit to your inadequacies? That may be our biggest weakness—failing to confess being weak. Most of the times I struggle, people don't know it. Oh, some do. Friends and family do. My wife does. God knows.

On the other hand, we should not revel in mediocrity. Neither should we strive for the lowest grade point average in our class. That would deny our stewardship and bring insult to our Lord. The biblical principle from 2 Corinthians 12 is *not* that we need to strive for weakness. The weakness is already there. The biblical principle to grab onto is whenever we are weak (and that's always), we are able to receive the grace of God and the power of God.

I like what N. T. Wright says about God's power in this context. He says:

> God's power and human power are not only not the same thing; often the second [human power] has to be knocked out of the way altogether for the first to shine through as God desires and intends . . . . [Paul] has discovered that there is a different kind of strength, the kind that's really worth having, and that to possess it you have to be weak.[4]

You may be familiar with the writings of Henri Nouwen and his mentor Jean Vanier, founder of the L'Arche communities—residential facilities for men and women with intellectual disabilities. Vanier tells the story of L'Arche resident Fabio who joined a group travelling to visit the Pope at the Vatican.

As the group awaited the Pope, Fabio, an energetic and active young man, bounded up to the Pope's throne and made himself comfortable. The assembly was shocked, but Fabio was content. He was free from the inhibitions that limit those with no such "intellectual weakness."[5]

We learn from the apostle Paul that weakness is a "badge of honor" for the Christian.[6] Weakness isn't something that we have to work at covering up. Would that we could have the freedom of Fabio and not be so worried about how our weakness may be evaluated by everyone else.

Up to this point in our consideration of human weakness, we have been focusing on strengths and abilities (or the lack of these). In addition to the countless human weaknesses, we must not ignore the universal struggle that even Christians have with what the Bible calls "the flesh"—our sinful nature (Rom. 7:5; Gal. 5:16). Briefly stated, the struggle that fallen human beings have with the sinful nature can be debilitating. The apostle Paul explains it this way: "I do not understand what I do. For what I want to do I do not do, but what I hate I do" (Rom. 7:15). In another text, he offers a similar description of the believer's internal war: "For the flesh desires what is contrary to the Spirit, and the Spirit what is contrary to the flesh. They are in conflict with each other, so that you are not to do whatever you want" (Gal. 5:17). It just may be that this innate spiritual weakness is the greatest threat that we face.

As long as we find ourselves in a fallen world on this side of heaven, we will continue to be challenged by the sinful nature. And when it comes to the matter of evaluating our personal strengths and abilities, we find ourselves especially susceptible to the sin of comparisons.

We may find life to be quite enjoyable and fulfilling until we compare ourselves to someone else. We could be very satisfied with a B for a paper or an exam until we learn that ours was the only B in the class, and all the other students received As. We may be okay with sitting on the bench as a freshman athlete until we learn that other freshmen are on the starting team. Third chair violin in the orchestra may be satisfactory until we discover that first chair players are not even music majors. We may be doing just fine until we observe how someone else has performed, and then our weakness becomes glaring, and our satisfaction is diminished.

In my interaction with college students, I have often initiated conversations about our human weakness and human brokenness. In the minds of most students there is the general assumption that everyone is doing okay. When we're asked, "How's it going?" and the universal response is, "Great"—we believe it, and so we conclude that we must be the only ones who are not okay. Embedded in evaluating our health and well-being is that nasty culprit of comparison. Whenever we compare our natural talent and ability with that of others, we will always find someone else who is stronger, smarter, or more capable.

Like Andrew from the beginning of this chapter felt his own weakness in the pursuit of excellent grades, we who live, work, and study in an academic community are especially vulnerable to the sin of comparing ourselves with others and concluding that we are either better or worse than our neighbors. But we are all weak—some of us just hide it more than others. None of us are perfect. Comparisons are irrelevant, and the achievement of perfection is impossible. We must acknowledge our weakness. And we must embrace God's grace and rely on God's power.

GOT GRACE?

If your situation is like that of the apostle Paul, then it is likely that you have prayed to have that thorn in the flesh extracted to overcome this personal weakness. But it remains. It's there for a purpose.

As Paul pleaded to have his thorn in the flesh removed, the Lord's answer wasn't "No, don't bother me." His answer was "No, there's something else I have for you—it's my grace." The Lord Jesus responded to the apostle, "My grace is sufficient for you, for my power is made perfect in weakness" (2 Cor. 12:9).

Paul came to a place in his prayer life where he received God's answer. Paul refers to having pleaded "three times" for the thorn's removal. But the pleading is past. It's over. The Lord has given the apostle an answer, and Paul has accepted that answer.

After Paul accepts God's answer, his struggle turns a corner, and he is living with a new and confident assurance that God's power will enable him to do what needs to be done. The greater our human weakness is, the more noticeable is the grace and the power of God.

I don't know the specific thing in your life that you may

consider to be a weakness. While I'm not suggesting that you bare your soul to everyone, I am suggesting that—in the right context, in a safe place, with a trusted prayer partner—sharing your weakness may be a good, necessary, and important step in your spiritual formation. In any case, the acknowledgement of weakness that is absolutely necessary is our acknowledgement of weakness to God. It is when we humbly bow before God, in prayer, in recognition of our weakness and God's power, that we will receive from God the healing grace we need.

Let me tell you about a student named Michael. I first met Michael during his junior year, and it didn't take me long to conclude that he was a brilliant and gifted student. When Michael applied for a position as student chaplain, I was delighted at the prospect of contributions he could make to the student body. Each year, I worked closely with four upperclassmen (two male and two female) who served their fellow students in spiritual life programming on campus.

During Michael's student chaplaincy as a senior, his leadership was readily apparent. On one occasion, his peers selected Michael to speak at an all-school communion. This was an opportunity for a student leader to offer a fifteen-minute message to students gathered for worship. I was stunned by the sophistication of that short but solid presentation that sounded more like an experienced professional than an untrained amateur.

Sometime later, I followed up with Michael to critique that message. Of course, my evaluation had nothing to do with any shortcoming in his talk. Quite the contrary. My counsel to Michael on that day had to do with confidence. Gently and sincerely I encouraged Michael to be aware of his own weakness (in spite of his gigantic gifts) and his need to grow, his need to learn, and his need to embrace the grace of God and the power of God in all of his endeavors. I shared with Michael my personal practice of praying for "confidence"—not confidence in myself, but confidence in Christ. I suggested to Michael that affirming our limitations and brokenness can help us find only what God can give: sufficient grace.

What is sufficient grace? It is grace that is "enough." It's what is adequate. It's just what we need. It's God's power made perfect in weakness. It's what the apostle Paul experienced. And it's what we can know as well: "When I am weak, then I am strong" (2 Cor. 12:10).

I find it interesting and instructive that Paul did not pray for grace, but he received it anyway. It was supplied to the apostle, and it is supplied to us—sufficient grace. It may come in the moment of a crisis, over the course of a semester, when we don't know how to pray as the Spirit intercedes on our behalf, or when we don't even know that we need it—sufficient grace.

FINALE

What a privilege it would be for us to come to the end of our lives and have the Lord explain how our weaknesses were used for our good and God's glory. And somehow, God saw those weaknesses and didn't correct them. In fact, God made us with those weaknesses, but God added His power and grace. What that will look like in your life and my life, I'm not exactly sure. But I do know that it will be good. It will be enough. Because the Lord Jesus said, "My grace is sufficient for you" (2 Cor. 12:9).

A Step Further

- *Who do you find yourself trying to be like? In what way?*

- *In what ways have you tried to hide weakness?*

- *How do you feel remembering that God knows every weakness you have?*

- *Does culture value weakness or strength? Does God value weakness or strength?*

- *Take ten minutes and write down any weakness you can think of—spiritual, emotional, physical. Then after each one, write down the words "My grace is sufficient for you."*

There is another kind of perfectionism
that is worth our attention and pursuit:
a pursuit of Christ and a contentment no
matter what our circumstances.

Chapter Three

Perfectionism—Friend or Foe?

I grew up watching a lot of baseball, and from a young age, I was familiar with the name Don Larsen. Larsen became a hero and a legend for pitching a "perfect game" in a World Series—something that no one had ever done before and something that no one has ever done since. It was game five of the World Series between the New York Yankees and the Brooklyn Dodgers on October 8, 1956. Throwing a "perfect game" means that Yankee pitcher Don Larsen held the Brooklyn team to no hits, no runs, no walks, no hit batsmen, and no Dodgers reaching first base. Larsen's performance was perfection—it was priceless.

But besides a spectacular performance in one game, Larsen was a rather non-descript player. One sports writer summarizes the rest of Don Larsen's baseball career as consisting of "unbroken mediocrity punctuated with flashes of competence."[1]

I don't suppose any of us would aspire to a life of "unbroken mediocrity," and yet few can claim to have achieved any sort of "perfection." The singular accomplishment of a New York Yankee pitcher on one October day demonstrates the rarity and elusiveness of perfection.

TYRANNY OF THE SHOULDS

Perfection is an unrealistic goal, to be sure. I think we would all enthusiastically agree. Yet we often put pressure on ourselves to achieve that goal and consider anything falling short to be failure. So when our efforts fall short and we fail at perfection, we can be awfully hard on ourselves. It's called "perfectionism."

In corresponding with a recent college graduate, I inquired about his life as a student. I asked Richard, "What helped, and what hurt? What would you like to pass along to students who are struggling to find their way through the college years?"

His response surprised me. But the more I thought about it, the more his words resonated with truth and wisdom. Richard focused on a phrase that he picked up in a psychology course, an idea from the writings of the German psychiatrist Karen Horney. It's the concept of the "tyranny of the shoulds"—and it's at the very heart of unrealistic perfectionism.[2]

Richard described his personal struggle with academics as a comparison game. Comparing himself with others regularly led to falling short of where he "should be." This led Richard to believe that he wasn't smart enough, and he wasn't good enough. For him, the "tyranny of the shoulds" was exhausting and painful. His advice to students—avoid it at all costs, "the tyranny of the shoulds."

I think Richard might be on to something.

PERFECTING OURSELVES TO DEATH

The college years are often distinguished by intense pressures to perform, to produce, and to perfect. Not that these pressures are absent before or after years in higher education, but the credential-seeking season of preparation for graduate school or vocational placement seems to exacerbate the dilemma.

Dr. Richard Winter, a British psychiatrist who taught for years at Covenant Seminary in St. Louis, has written a book on the subject of perfectionism. It's entitled *Perfecting Ourselves to Death: The Pursuit of Excellence and the Perils of Perfectionism.*[3] I like Dr. Winter's very practical and commonsense kind of approach to this topic, where he makes the distinction between a "healthy" type of perfectionism and an "unhealthy perfectionism." He's honest and transparent about his personal struggles. In his book, he confesses that his own tendencies toward an unhealthy perfectionism may be revealed in the extended delay of the publishing of his book. It seemed that there was always more to say, there were always revisions to be made to write the perfect book on perfectionism.[4] How ironic!

Perfectionism is indeed a mixed bag. There's a sense in which perfectionism is a good thing. Dr. Winter speaks autobiographically when he says, "In my own family there is a strong influence of what I consider to be healthy perfectionism, shown in the value that is placed on hard work, high standards, punctuality, cleanliness, tidiness, moral integrity, and maintaining good relationships."[5] If we are willing to grant that these traits could be classified as "perfectionistic" and healthy when they are not taken to an extreme—I'm sure that we can agree with Dr. Winter on this point.

Then, on the flip side—for "unhealthy perfectionism," Winter lists the following: "unrealistically high standards, low self-esteem, seek to excel at any cost, generalize failure, controlling, exhausted and exhausting."[6]

I don't know which category you fall into, but I know that there are times that I struggle very significantly with an unhealthy perfectionism—just ask my family. And I know that I am not alone in this. All too common is a perfectionism associated with hugely debilitating behaviors like anxiety, depression, eating disorders, obsessive-compulsive behavior, and relationship issues. While a certain kind of perfectionism can be good and healthy, there is another kind of perfectionism that painfully sabotages our health and well-being.

So, where do we go from here? How can we sort out the good from the bad and bring some sanity to our lives? What does God expect of us? I believe the Scriptures provide guidance to steady our emotions and keep us on track. There are two biblical texts that are important for us to consider: Matthew 5:43–48 and Philippians 4:11–13.

ASPIRING TO PERFECTION: MATTHEW 5:43–48

In part of Jesus' famous Sermon on the Mount He makes this stunning statement: "Be perfect, therefore, as your heavenly Father is perfect" (Matt. 5:48). You say, "There it is! A proof text for perfectionism!" Here's the whole text, Matthew 5:43–48:

> **"You have heard that it was said, 'Love your neighbor
> and hate your enemy.' But I tell you, love your ene-
> mies and pray for those who persecute you, that you
> may be children of your Father in heaven. He causes
> his sun to rise on the evil and the good, and sends
> rain on the righteous and the unrighteous. If you
> love those who love you, what reward will you get?
> Are not even the tax collectors doing that? And if you
> greet only your own people, what are you doing more
> than others? Do not even pagans do that? Be perfect,
> therefore, as your heavenly Father is perfect."**

To be sure, some have taken verse 48 as a proof text
for moral perfectionism. It's a text that has been used and
abused in all kinds of ways. But, as you know, whenever
we read Scripture, we need to interpret the meaning of the
words in the light of their context; and for this text, context
is especially important.

I want to be quick to confess that capable and orthodox
biblical scholars differ in their interpretations of this text.
In this case, one's understanding of the word "therefore" is
pivotal. If you believe "therefore" summarizes everything
Jesus has said up to this point in his sermon, then you will
interpret it one way.[7] If, instead, you believe "therefore"
summarizes just the last paragraph, beginning at verse 43,
then you will interpret the text another way.[8]

I am convinced of the latter view, that what Jesus is saying about "being perfect" has to do with the perfect love
that is exhibited by our heavenly Father. And this perfect
love is what Jesus is calling us to emulate.

Notice that in verse 45, Jesus describes the unique and
wonderful, all-embracing love of who? Our Father in

heaven. The theme of this paragraph is of loving our neighbor and our enemy, based on the love of our heavenly Father who loved us even when we were His enemies. As Scripture explains: "God demonstrates his own love for us in this: While we were still sinners, Christ died for us" (Rom. 5:8). This is the beauty of the love that God has for the world (John 3:16). God loves us not because of who we are but because of who He is.

Jesus is calling us to love even our enemies, even those who persecute us. And what kind of love is capable of that? Perfect love. It's God's kind of love. Jesus is calling us to show a perfect love—where we determine to love those who do not love us back. In fact, some language scholars point out that the Aramaic word that Jesus may well have spoken here is a word translated, not as "perfect," but as "all-embracing" or "all-including."[9]

Think with me for a moment about this radical kind of love that our Lord is calling us to. But what does this kind of love look like? How do we love our enemies? How can we love those who hate us?

Years ago, the Ford Motor Company produced a car called "Aspire." I've often laughed at that label adorning the body of an automobile—does it mean that this is not a real car, it's just aspiring to be one?[10] Other than a car model, the word "aspire" is a good one. This is what Matthew 5:48 is about. This is what you and I are about as we make attempts at living like Jesus, in loving like our heavenly Father. It is this kind of life and love to which we aspire.

There is something exciting that I see in this text. Jesus says, "Be perfect, therefore, as your heavenly Father is perfect." It's very subtle, but look at this with me carefully.

Notice that Jesus says "as your *heavenly Father* is perfect," not "as *God* is perfect." I think He chose this wording for a reason.

When Jesus speaks here of our heavenly Father's perfection, He is referring to what he has just said in verse 45 about our heavenly Father's love—shown to the righteous and the unrighteous. Just before that, He says those who love their enemies prove themselves to be children of the heavenly Father. Therefore, when Jesus says that we are to be perfect as our heavenly Father is perfect, He is saying implicitly that we can do it, but we don't do it alone. We can do it because we're God's children. We can do it because we have the family inheritance, we have the genes (so to speak), more accurately, we have the Holy Spirit to enable us.

Do you see it? Perfect love is beyond us, humanly speaking. Being human means we are not perfect—never were, and never will be in this life. But we who are children of the heavenly Father are enabled to do what a mere human being can never do. We can reveal our heavenly Father's character. We can love in a superhuman way. We can even love our enemies.

In this passage, Jesus links loving our enemies with praying for them. Dietrich Bonhoeffer is very practical when he explains in his book *The Cost of Discipleship*: "Through the medium of prayer we go to our enemy, stand by his side, and plead for him to God."[11]

Here is the mandate for perfection: only in the love of God and by the power of God are we called to aspire to perfection.

LEARNING CONTENTMENT:
PHILIPPIANS 4:11–13

The Matthew 5 text helps us in aspiring to a healthy perfection, a Christlike holiness. The Philippians 4 text guides us through our thorny world of imperfection by learning to live with contentment. We need divine assistance in both of these areas.

Whenever classes are in session, the college campus is a place of intense activity and the flow of people to the chaplain's office accelerates. Conversations with students, faculty, and staff reveal abundant needs from all directions within the entire campus community ranging from financial pressure to academic challenges to strict deadlines. Schedules bubble over, nerves are frayed, and stress is high. Everyone seems to be in a hurry. With so much to do and so little time to do it—one wonders if it all can really be accomplished, let alone with perfection. Into the mix of this busy, demanding, and need-filled environment comes the message of the Scriptures encouraging a life of "contentment."

In his letter to the Philippians, the apostle Paul concludes with a word of thanks to his Christian friends for their generous gift and genuine concern—followed by a word of testimony describing his personal contentment in the Lord in all circumstances. Here's what the apostle writes:

> **I have learned to be content whatever the circumstances. I know what it is to be in need, and I know what it is to have plenty. I have learned the secret of being content in any and every situation, whether well fed or hungry, whether living in plenty or in want. I can do all this through him who gives me strength.** (Phil. 4:11–13)

Even within as simple a thing as a "thank-you note," the apostle is teaching profound principles of God's providence and human contentment. And these are lessons worthy of our attention.

Jeremiah Burroughs, a seventeenth-century British Puritan, preached a series of sermons that were published in his book *The Rare Jewel of Christian Contentment.* He writes, "There is a great mystery and art in what way a Christian comes to contentment."[12] He closes with these words:

> I have spent many sermons over this lesson of contentment, but I am afraid that you will be longer in learning it than I have been preaching of it; it is a harder thing to learn it than it is to preach or speak of it.... Oh, do not be content with yourselves till you have learned this lesson of Christian contentment.[13]

What is most helpful to me as I read Paul's description of a "contented life" is that it is something "learned." So it is not automatic. It is not a gift. It is not a virtue that comes instantaneously at conversion. In verse 11, Paul says, "I have *learned* to be content whatever the circumstances." In verse 12 he says, "I have *learned* the secret of being content in any and every situation." This learning process is clearly something that happens over time and with experience. It doesn't come quickly. It doesn't come easily. And it doesn't come naturally.

This learning process that Paul is talking about is part of the sanctifying work of God in our lives. We who are enrolled in God's school of life enter into all kinds of experiences, and we learn from God how to trust Him. Contentment is not so much a "feeling" that we have while experiencing the vicissitudes of life; it is more—like the biblical sense of "shalom"—a condition of the soul, an environment of peace, even when the world around may be imperfect and chaotic.

The process of "learning" contentment varies from person to person, and it is especially important for those of us with a tendency toward unhealthy perfectionism that may include obsessive attention to all sorts of things. While Paul's word to his readers in Philippians 4 is not specifically addressing issues of perfectionism, he is urging his fellow believers to be satisfied with where they are, what they have, and what they don't have. In other words, we need to be content with less than perfection. We need to trust God in all circumstances and recognize His providential purposes.

There is a special set of contentment challenges for those of us who struggle with perfectionism. Some of us grapple with physical appearance matters—with body image or wardrobe—and those can leave us wounded and helpless. Some of us are stalled in our learning curve when it comes to relationships with friends or family, and we are easily hurt and left lonely. Some of us are confused most about intellectual ability or athletic talent, and we wonder about the fairness of giftedness. Some of us are frustrated most by an uncertain future, not knowing God's will for our lives.

What is it that challenges you most in this area of contentment? When our heart's desire is for perfection, how do you embrace contentment in an imperfect world? Because God is God—sovereign and in control—we have every reason to trust Him and live a life of contentment.

As we think about contentment and study Paul's teaching here in Philippians 4, it is interesting to observe the apostle's choice of this word "content." The Greek word is found as an adjective only here in the New Testament and as a noun in only two other New Testament texts.[14] What is fascinating is that Paul chose to use a word that was commonly used by the stoic philosophers of the day. For the stoic, contentment meant "self-sufficiency." A first-century Roman stoic may well have written something sounding much like Paul. In fact, one such stoic wrote this: "The happy man is content with his present lot, no matter what it is, and is reconciled to his circumstances."[15]

At this point, we need to press the pause button and underscore the distinction between the stoic life and the Christian life. In the biblical call to contentment, the Scriptures are not encouraging a fatalistic acceptance of "que sera, sera"—whatever will be, will be. The Old and New Testaments call us to strive for a God-honoring life—a sacrificial life of loving God and neighbor. The Scripture says, "Whatever you do, work at it with all your heart, as working for the Lord, not for human masters" (Col. 3:23). In academics, a believer studies hard for good grades in the faithful stewardship of God's gifts. In vocation, the Christ follower works with passion and energy as a divine calling. In all things, we pursue excellence as God gives us strength.

So Paul takes a strictly secular concept and turns it upside down. Paul turns "self-sufficiency" into "Christ-sufficiency." Paul's words to the Philippians encourage contentment along with accomplishment. In verse 13 the apostle says, "For I can do everything through Christ, who gives me strength" (NLT). Let's not miss the importance of this verse as it relates to contentment. Paul's meaning is without question—he confesses that his contentment and his strength for living are found ultimately and invariably in Christ. Again, it is not *self*-sufficiency that he advocates, it is *Christ*-sufficiency.

For those of us who never seem to be satisfied with who we are or how we are doing, this Christ-sufficient contentment can bring a sigh of relief and a newfound joy.

THOMAS KELLY: AN IMPERFECT LIFE

Thomas Kelly was born on a farm near Chillicothe, Ohio, in 1893, and raised in a Quaker family.[16] Kelly became a respected scholar and Quaker theologian whose works are still published and frequently quoted, especially his most well-known book *A Testament of Devotion*.[17]

After completing an undergraduate degree at Haverford College in Pennsylvania and a doctorate at Hartford Theological Seminary, Kelly and his wife moved from college to college for various teaching posts before finally returning to Haverford.

By the time Kelly returned to Haverford, he had completed work on a second doctorate at Harvard. With his coursework and dissertation writing finished, his oral defense was all that remained. But in his meeting with the Harvard faculty, Kelly's mind went blank—he failed the oral defense. Tragically, he was never allowed a second chance, and this horrific failure left Kelly devastated. It was 1937, and Kelly was forty-four years old. He was heartbroken and inconsolable.

Later that same year, after his great disappointment, Kelly experienced a life-changing encounter with God. His son put it like this:

There is no exact record of what happened in the following weeks, but it is certain that sometime during the months of November or December, 1937, a change was wrought within the very foundation of his soul.... Stripped of his defenses and human self-justification, he found, for the first time, a readiness to accept the outright gift of God's Love, and he responded with unlimited commitment to that leading.[18]

Thomas Kelly lived for only three more years after that remarkable healing that changed his life. His teaching and writing were transformed as he lived a new life of Christian contentment. In his own words, "I have been literally melted down by the love of God."[19]

Kelly's life was not a perfect life. In fact, it was marked by significant imperfection. But the love of God meant all the difference in the world. And contentment filled his soul.

FRIEND OR FOE?

There is a kind of perfectionism that is an enemy—an unhealthy and detrimental foe. God does not call us to that kind of perfect living that brings anxiety or depression or any number of other hurtful symptoms. But there is another kind of perfectionism that is worth our attention and pursuit. It is a pursuit of excellence, yes, but even more than that, it is a pursuit of Christ and a contentment no matter what our circumstances. With God's help, we can strive for that kind of perfection.

A Step Further

- *In what areas do you struggle with the idea of perfectionism?*

- *How does the perfection of Christ help us in our imperfection?*

- *In what ways could you better love others around you, even your enemies?*

- *In what ways are you least content?*

- *How do you try to control outcomes? Do you let God in on all of your decisions?*

- *How can you be more content without being apathetic?*

- *When you think of a contented person, who comes to mind?*

It's trusting in the promises of God
and affirming the goodness
of God that have kept God's people
going over the generations.

Chapter Four

Dual Dilemmas—Doubt and Depression

The title of psychiatrist Richard Kadison's book says it all: *College of the Overwhelmed*.[1] The longer I served in ministry on the college campus, spending untold hours in the company of students, the more I could validate Kadison's observations about the mental health struggles of college and university students. In returning to his book time and again, I have found myself in agreement that all too many students do indeed find themselves enrolled in the "College of the Overwhelmed."

Dr. Kadison directed Mental Health Services at Harvard University and specialized in student mental health treatment. He explains how the undergraduate college years are often not as fun and carefree as some might suppose. Beneath the veneer of a life of ease and comfort, college students face a host of mental health challenges.

As students experience all kinds of stressors in their

navigation of academics, relationships, and personal identity, troubling symptoms bubble to the surface:

- depression
- sleep disorders
- substance abuse
- anxiety disorders
- eating disorders
- impulsive behaviors[2]

The subtitle of Kadison's book is *The Campus Mental
Health Crisis and What to Do about It.* The solutions that Dr.
Kadison proposes are helpful and practical as they deal with
educational programs and mental health services. However,
one resource that Dr. Kadison does not address in his book
is the resource of any religious faith. I really didn't expect
him to address life's spiritual dimension, but it certainly
would have been in order. In this chapter, we will use Kadison's general mental health observations as a springboard
into a study of spiritual matters of the soul.

DOUBT AND DEPRESSION
CONSIDERED TOGETHER?

Maybe you're wondering about the wisdom of connecting
these two similar but dissimilar struggles. For our purposes
here, the similarities outweigh the differences as both doubt
and depression impact mental and spiritual health. Also,
the dynamics of the two are profound—since doubt may
lead to depression and vice versa.

You might say that in our consideration of "doubt," we

will be focusing on the emotional side of doubt rather than the intellectual side of doubt. With intellectual doubt we wrestle with philosophical, historical, or scientific objections to our Christian faith. Emotional doubt relates to one's feelings, one's mental state in the midst of a struggle with certainty. Emotional doubt describes one's mood that persists regardless of the preponderance of evidence or the persuasiveness of argument.

While emotional doubt and intellectual doubt are inextricably related, the focus of our consideration of doubt in this chapter is on the feeling orientation of doubt—and in fact, our study here will be linking the dual emotional dilemmas of doubt and depression. Intellectual matters of faith that lead to doubt are better addressed in a study of apologetics which is beyond the scope of this book.

Doubt and depression are human conditions that may blindside otherwise healthy people. From a Christian perspective and a more holistic approach, we need to address the twin struggles of doubt (spiritual) and depression (psychological) in our quest for health and well-being. Coupling psychological and biblical resources will provide help and hope for people of faith.

COUNSELING BY THE BOOK

In my ministry of pastoral care and counseling, my most valuable resource is the Bible. Whatever life situation or problem students might bring to me, there are always biblical principles or specific texts of Scripture that can be carefully and thoughtfully shared. These Scriptures are not dispensed as pills from a bottle; they are carefully introduced in the context of caring conversation, pastoral understanding, and compassionate prayer.

As I met with students, faculty, and staff for conversation and prayer concerning the various struggles, fears, and challenges, I often turned to the Psalms. Time and again I found that the Psalms speak to the "hard issues" and the "heart issues" of human life. I want to give specific attention to Psalm 13 which has wide application to a great number of issues, specifically, doubt and depression.

Psalm 13 is a great resource for those of us enrolled in the "college of the overwhelmed"—and frankly, who isn't at one point or another? Here is a biblical text that speaks to our condition. It may seem unusual to consult a three-thousand year-old document to address life in the twenty-first century, but the Scriptures have demonstrated value in every age, as human nature changes little over time. The problems facing King David in ancient Israel are remarkably similar to issues confronting you and me today.

From the heading, we see that this is a psalm of David. But the heading also says, "For the Director of Music," signaling its use in the worshiping community. While the original author is describing personal feelings associated with specific life experiences, the application is far greater; it's a psalm to be read or prayed or sung in community worship.

This psalm comes out of anguish; it's the expression of a suffering and weary heart. It's a short psalm, only 6 verses, with a message intended for those who know the anxiety of doubt and the pain of depression.

> How long, LORD? Will you forget me forever?
> How long will you hide your face from me?

> **How long must I wrestle with my thoughts**
> **and day after day have sorrow in my heart?**
> **How long will my enemy triumph over me?**
> **Look on me and answer, LORD my God.**
> **Give light to my eyes, or I will sleep in death,**
> **and my enemy will say, "I have overcome him,"**
> **and my foes will rejoice when I fall.**
> **But I trust in your unfailing love;**
> **my heart rejoices in your salvation.**
> **I will sing the LORD'S praise,**
> **for he has been good to me.** (Ps. 13:1–6)

These words of David are a poignant expression of an individual lament.[3] The laments in the Psalms are forthright and sometimes brutal statements of pain and objection brought against God. There's a complaint here. It's a bold challenge to heaven, "How long, LORD?" Four times David says it, "How long, how long, how long, how long?" With these questions, the psalmist is expressing his sorrow in feeling abandoned by God. When God seems absent, our emotions are dark as the world closes in. Have you ever felt like this? Have you ever asked God, "Where are you?"

David is struggling. It's a life and death situation, and the pain is real. There is tension here. There are tears here. This is what I appreciate about the Psalms: real expressions by real people in search of real answers.

The emotions expressed here in Psalm 13 are real emotions. And if we can learn anything from this psalm, it's a lesson encouraging honesty with God. Here we are freed to be open before God. Even our closest friends might not understand our questions of anguish and our cries of complaint—but God does. And when our experience in life leaves us feeling that God has abandoned us, our feelings are fully understood by the one who matters most—the God we so dearly want to be close to and the God who so dearly wants to be close to us.

THE DILEMMA OF DOUBT

One issue I have discussed with students time and again on the college campus is "doubt." It's a concern that should and must be addressed. The Bible doesn't ignore it, and neither should we. Here in Psalm 13 we find the psalmist David, the man after God's own heart (1 Sam. 13:14; Acts 13:22), approaching God with all of his doubts and fears.

Doubt is not the same thing as unbelief. This we must be careful to distinguish. Doubt stands between belief and unbelief. The English word "doubt" comes from the Latin *dubitare* meaning "two." You might say that "to doubt" means trying to hold onto two things at once—belief and unbelief. Doubting is pictured in Chinese culture as someone having one foot in one boat and the other foot in another boat.[4] That's a precarious position—a position I recently experienced at the lake—with one foot in the boat and one foot on the dock (almost splitting my pants).

In Psalm 13, David is distressed with the hiddenness of God:

> How long, LORD? Will you forget me forever?
> How long will you hide your face from me?
> How long must I wrestle with my thoughts
> and day after day have sorrow in my heart?
> How long will my enemy triumph over me?

Then in verses 3 and 4, David seeks God:

> **Look on me and answer, LORD my God.**
> **Give light to my eyes, or I will sleep in death;**
> **and my enemy will say, "I have overcome him,"**
> **and my foes will rejoice when I fall.**

It is reported that "the dying French atheist Voltaire said, 'I am abandoned by God and man.'"[5] And while David opens his psalm by raising a serious complaint against God about feeling abandoned, we can see that this calling God to account is not the railing of an unbeliever. David's distraught words in verses 1 and 2 and prayerful words in verses 3 and 4 are issued from a person of faith, one whose faith is serious and genuine.

As in many of the psalms of David, there is reference in Psalm 13 to an "enemy." In verse 2, David asks, "How long will my enemy triumph over me?" In verse 4, David says, "My enemy will say, 'I have overcome him,' and my foes will rejoice when I fall." Of course, there is no way of knowing exactly what the psalmist is considering to be his enemy in these verses. It may have been Saul and/or other opponents;[6] the enemy could be the personification of death;[7] or as some have thought—the enemy may be the sinful nature or Satan himself.[8]

Could it be that David's real enemy is doubting that God cares? In the midst of all that overwhelms, it just may be that the most troubling of matters is our forgetting that the almighty God of the universe is a personal God who cares and is present. It could be that doubt is plaguing us as an enemy stealing our joy and leaving us feeling abandoned and alone. The enemy of doubt.

THE DILEMMA OF DEPRESSION

Depression, of course, comes in all shapes and sizes for all kinds of reasons. And some depressions are entirely beyond our understanding and our control. There are plenty of conditions that require the help of medical professionals, the prescription of anti-depressant medications, or the assistance of trained therapists. As a college chaplain, I always had a close working relationship with the student health center and the student counseling center. Those two offices were on my speed-dial, and I had their permission to escort a student without an appointment for their services.

David's enemy of doubt leads to the related dilemma of depression. It seems like some form of depression is plaguing the psalmist as he composes Psalm 13. In verse 2 he says, "How long must I wrestle with my thoughts and day after day have sorrow in my heart?" In verse 3 he says, "Give light to my eyes, or I will sleep in death." These verses could very well be using metaphorical language in describing a seriously debilitating depression. We don't know the precise nature of David's emotional condition in Psalm 13, but we may well identify with his symptoms of suffering.

Let me tell you about Robert, a recent college graduate who entered the work world as a high school math and science teacher. Robert had a career in his field of study and a serious girlfriend. Things were going well. Then depression hit, out of nowhere, with no apparent incident or cause— just deep, dark depression.

Robert fought the depression by reading books and talking to friends. But when the dark feelings persisted, he sought the help of a physician who referred him to a psychiatrist. The psychiatrist suggested the possibility of a chemical imbalance of some kind. Medication lifted his spirits, but Robert resisted being dependent on pills and took his medication only sporadically.

As the months rolled by, the heavy mood began to affect Robert's spiritual life, and he started questioning the validity of Christian faith. He bravely sought the counsel of a pastor and pressed for an explanation to unanswered prayer. Maybe he didn't have enough faith. Maybe he wasn't really a Christian. Maybe there isn't a God out there. These questions were sincere concerns of a sincere heart—and with pastoral counsel, Robert began to see hope for the future.

In Robert's story, there was a definitive point of turnaround. With the pastor's counsel from the gospel account of Jesus' healing at the pool of Bethesda (John 5:1–15), Robert's eyes were opened. Jesus' question to the man who had gone so long without help was a simple one, "Do you want to get well?" (John 5:6). With that question, and with a commitment in prayer to do whatever was necessary, Robert determined that he did indeed want to get well.

A new course was set and new steps were taken. Back to the psychiatrist with a willingness to take the prescribed meds. Back to the pastor with Robert's promise to engage in specific spiritual exercises including: devotions in the Psalms, memorization of Scripture, a plan for journaling, and regular prayer with a small group.

Robert survived that eleven month season that began as the bleakest stretch of time he had ever experienced. With the help of caring, trained professionals in medicine and ministry, Robert gained some insight and tools for the battle. Now he knows a little more about mental and spiritual health, and he knows how important it is to have an answer to the question, "Do you want to get well?"

David, we will see in Psalm 13, also found a source of help. His answer came in a decisive step of faith. This description of moving from fog to faith, through an episode of doubt and depression, has proved to be a healing pattern for men and women struggling with similar trials today.

As dark and dreary as this psalm may seem in the first four verses, the last stanza closes with a word of hope. David did not struggle as someone who had no hope—and neither should we. David writes:

> **But I trust in your unfailing love;**
> **my heart rejoices in your salvation.**
> **I will sing the LORD's praise,**
> **for he has been good to me.**

Even though David complains that in his heart he feels the absence of God, he is able to move beyond his feelings, to the reality he knows to be true. For a moment, he is able to take his eyes off of the wind and waves, and he grabs hold of that hope which is an anchor for his soul that holds him firm and secure (see Heb. 6:19). The Lord is our hope. He is our anchor.

Biblical hope is more than wishful thinking—it's more than a vague hunch that everything is going to be okay. "I hope the new professor is an easy grader" is just a wish. "I hope the football team wins on Saturday" is just a wish. Again, from the book of Hebrews we read, "Let us hold unswervingly to the hope we profess, for he who promised is faithful" (Heb. 10:23). A good definition of biblical hope could be worded like this: Hope is a confident assurance in the promises of God. Ultimately, our hope is in a Person, and that Person is God. The God of hope is not some mystical theory. Our God is the God of hope (Rom. 15:13). And this is the truth that David affirms when he writes: "But I trust in your unfailing love; my heart rejoices in your salvation" (Ps. 13:5).

There's no indication that in Psalm 13, when we get to verses 5 and 6 that the storm is over. But there's a new found sense of security seen in these closing verses of Psalm 13, and that security comes in the promises of God. Deliverance from the enemy has not yet come. When and how that deliverance may arrive, God only knows. But in the meantime, David says, "I trust in your unfailing love."

It's true in the Old Testament, it's true in the New Testament, and it's true today. In Psalm 13 it's the divine attribute of the Hebrew word *hesed* translated as "unfailing love" (in verse 5) that keeps David going. Our Lord is committed to His people; His love is loyal. So we remember those promises and hold fast to them in faith, especially in times of doubt or depression. Just as bars or straps are provided for standing passengers on commuter trains, believers grab onto the promises of God for safety and security.

The German pastor and theologian Dietrich Bonhoeffer wrote this prayer:

> In me there is darkness, but with thee there is light.
> I am lonely, but thou leavest me not.
> I am restless, but with thee there is peace. Amen.[9]

It's trusting in the promises of God and affirming the goodness of God that have kept God's people going over the generations. No, we may not understand all that we're going through or why it is happening. But that doesn't mean that God is absent or asleep.

HOW MUCH FAITH IS ENOUGH?

When it comes to struggling with doubt and depression—let's not be too hard on ourselves for weakness or failure. Do you the remember the gospel account of Jesus walking on water followed by Peter walking on water (Matt. 14:22–33)? You'll recall that Peter's water-walk didn't go so well. Jesus reached out and rescued the sinking disciple, "'You of little faith,' he said, 'why did you doubt?'" (Matt. 14:31). Indeed, Peter had little faith. But he had faith. Here, in this one man on this one occasion, we see faith *and* we see doubt. I think that the Swiss theologian Ulrich Luz says it best with this word of pastoral counsel: "All faith has 'little faith' in it, and . . . doubt is part of human faith."[10]

Another Swiss author, physician Paul Tournier, offers some insight into this astute observation that authentic faith need not be completely free from doubt, since doubt is part of the condition of not seeing (Heb. 11:1). In Tournier's book *To Resist or To Surrender?*, Dr. Tournier writes, "Faith would no longer be faith if there no longer remained any possibility of doubt."[11] He explains, "[The one] who claims never to have doubted does not know what faith is, for faith is forged through doubt."[12]

Douglas Nelson tells the story of a visit he made to an English castle containing a dungeon with a tiny cell that held an incredible history. When in use, this little prison cell was entirely devoid of light. Now—illuminated for all to see—a stone wall was exposed, revealing a crack where desperately thirsty prisoners had licked the moisture coming in from the castle moat. Remarkably, a sentence had been carved into the stone wall. Possibly with a belt buckle, someone had inscribed the words of Jacob from Genesis 28:16, "The Lord was in this place and I knew it not."[13]

Even in the darkness of our worst prisons, the Lord is with us. We don't always *feel* that. In fact, it can seem to be quite the contrary. An academic career can feel like enrollment in the "College of the Overwhelmed." But with the promises of God throughout the Scriptures, we can join the psalmist in affirming to our Lord, "I trust in your unfailing love." In our mind's eye, maybe we can transfer to a college where we are "overwhelmed by the love of God."

In Romans 15:13, the apostle Paul prayed, "May the God of hope fill you with all joy and peace as you trust in him, so that you may overflow with hope by the power of the Holy Spirit."

- -

A Step Further

- *When do you find yourself doubting?*

- *In what areas do you feel most depressed?*

- *What are God's promises in Psalm 13?*

- *What steps can you take to have greater faith in God's promises?*

- *Do you believe depression is just something one needs to live with? Why or why not?*

- *Do you believe it is wrong to take medication for help with depression? Why or why not?*

- *What are some spiritual resources that may be appropriate for depression?*

If Jesus gives us permission
to cease our doing, we can give
ourselves that same permission.

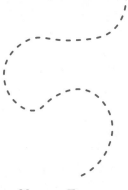

Chapter Five

An Unclaimed Gift—The Sabbath

Brooke entered my office well in advance of a committee meeting on both of our schedules. Her countenance revealed sadness, and I knew that she had something to discuss. It didn't take much prodding to learn that Brooke had just experienced a troubling encounter with a friend. They were passing each other between classes when Brooke stopped Suzanne to ask if she had time to talk. Brooke was hurt when Suzanne responded by checking her phone calendar and proposing a time the next day.

There's such a thing as being busy—but it rises to another level altogether when it hijacks our life and stands in the way of helping a friend in time of need.

THE CRISIS OF BUSYNESS

"How are you doing?" is a common question offered casually, almost unconsciously. Actually, it's more of a greeting than a question. What's your customary response to this greeting? Way too many times I have found myself answering, "I'm busy." I've noticed friends and acquaintances seem to be quite fond of that response as well.

We live busy lives in a busy environment, in a busy culture, in a busy world. With our frenzied schedules, we aim at fitting all too much into 24 hours. If we're honest, we need to confess just being too busy. Life in our modern world is complicated and overcrowded. Duties and obligations urge us to produce more and more. In Japan, they use an apt expression, *karoshi*, which means "death from overwork."[1] But the pressures are not all external. The internal pressure of drivenness pushes us. The fear of failure haunts us. It's a weary way to live. Maybe you feel this way right now.

Pastor and author John Ortberg tells the story of a conversation that he had with a wise friend and spiritual mentor as John was seeking guidance in beginning a new and demanding ministry. Ortberg phrased the question this way: "What do I need to do to be spiritually healthy?" After a long pause on the telephone line, the answer came back, "You must ruthlessly eliminate hurry from your life." After another long pause, John said, "Okay, I've written that one down, that's a good one. Now what else is there?" There was another long pause as John waited for an additional spiritual gem. But no further advice was given. Ortberg's mentor said, "There is nothing else, you must ruthlessly eliminate hurry from your life."[2] That mentor knew John and knew what he needed to hear.

The problem is busyness, hurry. What's the solution? Some are tempted to numb the pressure of busyness and the constant demand to produce with medication or amusements that take away the pain.

In this chapter I am proposing a divine prescription for the unhealthy reality that too many of us are living in when we worship our work, forget the worship of God, and ignore the need of rest for body, mind, and spirit.

A DIVINE PRESCRIPTION

How might we be guilty of worshiping our work? The term "workaholic" is familiar to those in the work world who "take their work home with them" even with a sense of pride for a 24/7 devotion to employment. But workaholism isn't limited to life beyond college and those drawing a paycheck in the workforce. Students can worship their "work" of academics or athletics or other activities that consume their focus and energy.

So here's the dilemma: Can we be satisfied with studying or working within reasonable limits? Must we "burn the candle at both ends" in order to complete our tasks and do our best? Or is there another way? Is there a divine prescription and a divine perspective allowing us to rest in the sovereignty of God?

We need to think seriously about an old remedy to our contemporary plight. It's an ancient remedy that goes back to the Old Testament. But in it, we find something that is new, refreshing, and healing. The fourth commandment in Exodus 20 says:

> **Remember the Sabbath day by keeping it holy. Six days you shall labor and do all your work, but the seventh day is a sabbath to the LORD your God. On it you**

shall not do any work, neither you, nor your son or daughter, nor your male or female servant, nor your animals, nor any foreigner residing in your towns. For in six days the LORD made the heavens and the earth, the sea, and all that is in them, but he rested on the seventh day. Therefore the LORD blessed the Sabbath day and made it holy. (Ex. 20:8–11)

I don't know how recently you may have read this commandment or considered its application to twenty-first-century life. Sabbath-keeping is not on most people's "to do" list. But it should be.

Any attempt to apply the fourth commandment to today is distinctly countercultural. Americans have come to understand Sunday as just another Saturday or just another workday. In the era before online purchasing, I remember that counting the number of shopping days before Christmas required subtracting Sundays when stores would be closed. Now, Sundays are some of the busiest and most important days for merchants. Not to promote or prohibit Sunday shopping—I'm just saying that our 24/7 consumerism has become one more push to produce. All of the buying is part of all of the doing that prevents us from any kind of rest.

In the fourth commandment we receive a divine perspective on work and rest. God created us to work hard and then rest. We rest not just to get re-energized for more work, but in our rest we acknowledge that God is in control. God can bless our six-day effort, and God can keep the world going quite well without our 24/7 production.

The biblical concept of Sabbath rescues human beings from all of our human doing—because at the heart of the

Sabbath is the provision of *rest*. The Hebrew noun *shabbat* (English *Sabbath observance*) is related to the Hebrew verb *shabat* which literally means "to cease, rest, or stop."[3] Israel observed the Sabbath day on Saturday, the seventh day of the week.

The reason I believe so strongly in observing the Sabbath is because of the way this commandment is presented in Scripture. When God gives to Moses the command, "Remember the Sabbath day by keeping it holy," our Lord grounds that commandment on the fact that on the seventh day, the Creator rested. Exodus 20:11 says, "For in six days the LORD made the heavens and the earth, the sea, and all that is in them, but he rested on the seventh day. Therefore the LORD blessed the Sabbath day and made it holy." Why did God rest on the seventh day? Because He was tired? No—an omnipotent God doesn't get tired. Did God rest because He was tapped out and couldn't think of anything else to do? No—an omniscient God doesn't lose creativity. God rested on the seventh day as a pattern for His image-bearers, you and me. In creation, God designed the model of work and rest.

THE TEACHING OF JESUS: SABBATH AS A GIFT

Now here's the key—rest is a gift of God, given to weary people. And interestingly enough, it is a commandment of God. Rest is not only something that God *allows*, but it is something that God *commands*. The fourth commandment was written in stone by the finger of God, intended for human living and human thriving.

Our best source of help concerning the question of the

Sabbath comes from Jesus Himself. Jesus confirmed the importance of the Sabbath, yet He condemned the legalism that surrounded it when He said, "'The Sabbath was made for man, not man for the Sabbath'" (Mark 2:27). Jesus spoke these words to the supreme legalists of His day, the Pharisees. The principle of the Sabbath is simple, but the rabbinical teaching of the day added detailed provisions—including thirty-nine categories of "work" prohibited on the Sabbath.[4]

The Pharisees of Jesus' day were masters at distorting the Scriptures, and one of their most abused targets was the fourth commandment. It was our Lord's intention to provide the Sabbath as a gift. It is a gift of rest, a gift for our good, a gift for our health and well-being. Yet all too often, it is a gift that we don't or won't receive.

The story is told of a minister in a north Georgia farming community who visited one of his parishioners. The two men stood along a fence-row and watched a new picking-machine roll through the cotton field. The minister said, "That's an amazing machine, picking six rows of cotton in minutes." "Yes it is," the farmer responded, "but I've got to tell you that I really do miss my mules." "Really? Why?" "Because these new picking-machines work day and night, every day. My mules worked only six days a week, and then they needed a rest, to have enough energy for the next week. When my mules rested, I rested. And I was better off for it."[5]

The Scriptures present the Sabbath principle as evidence of the grace of God. In a world filled with contradictory signals coming from every direction, our Lord brings a gracious invitation. Just as Jesus addressed the people of His day who were suffering under the enormous weight of legalism, Jesus says to us: "Come to me, all you who are weary and burdened, and I will give you rest. Take my yoke upon you and learn from me, for I am gentle and humble in heart, and you will find rest for your souls" (Matt. 11:28–29).

The rest we enjoy in the observance of a Sabbath is just part of the kind of rest that our Lord offers. What we find through faith in the Lord Jesus is a rest "for our souls." The New Testament describes "Sabbath rest" in the ultimate sense of salvation in Christ and life that is everlasting (Heb. 4:9–11). This rest comes in knowing that our sins are forgiven and there is no condemnation for God's children.

THE LEE PFUND STORY

Lee Pfund was a friend of mine, an older friend, born in 1919.[6] As a young man in his 20's, Lee began a professional baseball career. Back in the day, when American Christians were far more sensitive about Sabbath keeping, Lee signed his first professional baseball contract with a provision excusing him from Sunday games. Lee's Christian convictions required him to seek this exemption.

Lee joined the Cardinal organization in 1941; later he signed a major league contract with the Brooklyn Dodgers, and he played for other teams as well. In each case, the provision was made in his contract that he would not be required "to work," playing professional baseball, on Sunday.

These religious convictions concerning Sabbath observance actually led to an abbreviated career. You see, Lee was a pitcher, and one manager required him to pitch more frequently during the week since he was not pitching on Sunday. An arm-injury resulted, and his career was shortened. But in God's providence, Lee's abbreviated playing career was followed by a long and distinguished college coaching career.

I don't know of anyone today who would seek such an accommodation to Sabbath observance. And I think that we can agree that for Christ followers in the church, there should be no attempt to offer a long list of do's and don'ts concerning observance of the Lord's Day.

But at the same time, it seems to me that believers in the church should work with one another and help one another concerning the matter of observing the Sabbath in a way that honors God. Twenty-first century Christians seem to be very good at avoiding legalism. But in an effort to avoid legalism, the issue of the Sabbath has been avoided almost completely.

It cannot be emphasized too much that the Sabbath is a gift of God, and if there were ever a time when a Sabbath was needed, it's in today's busy world. But how can this happen without falling into pharisaical legalism? How can we be committed to Sabbath observance without coming across as "holier than thou?" We must find a way to be faithful to Scripture and to find the beauty and benefit of all that God intends.

KRISTEN'S TESTIMONY

Before exploring specific applications and ideas regarding Sabbath observance for twenty-first-century believers, let me share an experience of a college student I knew.

The encounter is vivid in my memory. As I walked out of the college library, a student approached me and introduced herself as Kristen. She explained that she was a sophomore, and she wanted to tell me about her experience with the Sabbath.

It had been seven or eight weeks since Kristen heard me give a talk on Sabbath observance, and she wanted to let me know how encouraged she was in her new-found practice of observing the Sabbath. She excitedly explained how rest and worship—without classes and without studying—lifted her spirits giving new energy and joy. Wow! Totally unsolicited, a sincere testimony.

Actually, Kristen wasn't the first nor the last person who has shared with me a similar story concerning help found in Sabbath observance. But it's so countercultural, that I am taken aback every time I hear such words of appreciation for the fourth commandment.

Observing the Sabbath provides time for personal rest and corporate worship that gives strength, energy, and joy for the other six days of the week. Where did that time come from? No extra time—still 168 hours in every week for every person. But the way we use one-seventh of that time can be life-changing.

"THE PAUSE THAT REFRESHES"

In 1929, the Coca-Cola company initiated an advertising campaign with the slogan, "the pause that refreshes." Coca-Cola understood that a pause from the busyness of life is indeed refreshing (especially with a Coke in hand).

We were created with a need for rest in body, mind, and spirit, and applying the Sabbath principle provides this personal pause. It's worth noting that the fourth commandment is not only a command to rest, but it is also a command to work. In Exodus 20:8–10 we read, "Remember the Sabbath day by keeping it holy. Six days you shall labor and do all your work, but the seventh day is a sabbath to the LORD your God."

When we are obedient to our Lord's command to work and to produce, then we also need to be obedient to our Lord's command to rest. We need a regular renewal of our physical bodies. It doesn't take a scientific study to prove the unhealthy consequences of inadequate rest. Fatigue, irritability, resentment, cynicism, and insomnia are just some of the unhappy factors accompanying insufficient rest.

Again, the word "Sabbath" means "to cease, rest, or stop." Resting on the Sabbath relates primarily to the work that we're doing on the other days of the week. It's the work that occupies us all week long that we are encouraged "to cease" on the Sabbath.

More than once I have had college students justify studying on Sunday by saying they were ceasing what they were doing on the other six days. I call that a "wise-guy" explanation! (Even if it happens to be true.)

Before going any further, we need to add a qualifier regarding Sunday work. There are some occupations—including police, fire, medical, and of course ministers—where Sunday work is required, and these Sunday workers need to find another day of the week to observe Sabbath rest.

Speaking very practically, for those who can observe a Sunday Sabbath but just haven't found it convenient, I encourage you to give it a try. However, for the sake of your health and sanity, don't quit your Sunday work cold-turkey. That could be disastrous. No matter where you are in all of this, I would offer a modest proposal of setting aside at least part of Sunday as a Sabbath time—a rest time, a renewal time, that is for your good and for God's glory.

There are a couple of things that happen when we choose to rest—to quit what we have been doing for the last six days. First, we catch our breath and experience a sense of relief. With all of the attention given to our work, a much-needed emotional healing comes with a break from those demands. Rest on the Sabbath can recharge our batteries. You can take a nap or go for a walk or a jog to the glory of God. With rest, we can clear the calendar to just *be* without having to *do*.

Secondly, when we observe a Sabbath as "the Lord's Day," we acknowledge what Jesus said about the Sabbath. Jesus said that He was the Lord of the Sabbath. Jesus is the Lord of the Sabbath, and He is the Lord of every other day as well. When on Sunday we rest from our work, we rest in the Lord. Sabbath rest soothes the soul. If Jesus gives us permission to cease our doing, we can give ourselves that same permission—freedom from doing.

There's one word found twice in the fourth commandment that we have yet to consider. It's the word *holy*. "Remember the Sabbath day by keeping it holy." After six days of creating, God rested. And the Scripture goes on to say, "Therefore the LORD blessed the Sabbath day and made it holy." *Holy* doesn't mean "super-spiritual" or "really religious." It simply means "set-apart," to be different. The Sabbath is intended to be different from the rest of the week. Work, worship, rest; work, worship, rest. It's a sacred rhythm. The Sabbath is part of that rhythm.

But how do we move from theory to practice? Ask

yourself this question: What stirs my affection for God? This shouldn't be something that creates more anxiety and frustration, but something that truly draws you closer to the Lord. Is it reading a book? Working out with headphones and music? Talking to a friend? Being outside in nature? Is it visiting hospital patients, serving in a ministry at your church, or serving at a homeless shelter in the city? It's different for each one of us. We can find that sweet spot that energizes our love for the Lord and for people.

As we embrace the Sabbath as time to rest in the Lord, we learn to relax in God. We grow in trusting God. In this sense, the Sabbath becomes an oasis that soothes the soul.

Maybe it's time to hit the pause button.

LET'S GET TOGETHER

In addition to the value of personal rest, applying the Sabbath principle prioritizes "corporate worship." The biblical injunction calling Christians to worship together as a body of believers is a familiar one—Hebrews 10:25: "And let us not neglect our meeting together, as some people do, but encourage one another, especially now that the day of his return is drawing near" (NLT).

Christian believers gather on the first day of the week to give to God their worship—adoration, praise, and thanksgiving—celebrating the one, true, living God: Father, Son, and Holy Spirit. As we commit ourselves to regular, weekly worship honoring the Creator, Redeemer, and Sustainer of life, we are reminded of the character of God and the character qualities that our Lord desires in us.

Pastor Bob Thune, in an article entitled, "Becoming

What We Behold," describes the difference between true worship and false worship along with the implications for everyday life. He provides this apt warning:

> When we worship false gods, we become like them.
> Our worship of money makes us greedy and stingy.
> Our worship of power makes us harsh and demanding.
> Our worship of approval makes us anxious and fearful.
> Our worship of success makes us busy and restless. The more we avert our gaze from the true God and chase these idols, the more ungodly we become.[7]

Such insight regarding worship applies to the corporate gathering of the people of God as well as the daily offering of our "bodies as a living sacrifice, holy and pleasing to God—this is your true and proper worship" (Rom. 12:1).

The Christian Sabbath is not intended to be a dull and boring day. It's a day for worship, for rest, for spiritual renewal. It's a day to celebrate with the people of God the resurrection of Jesus. It's a day that is a gracious gift from the hand of God. It's a day that is most important for people like you and me—people who are busy, and often *too* busy.

Thank God for the Sabbath.

A Step Further

- *On a scale of 1–10, how busy do you typically feel?*

- *When you think of the word "Sabbath"—what do you think of?*

- *Do you take a day for "Sabbath"?*

- *What kinds of activities stir your affections for Jesus? What kinds of activities create anxiety and stress?*

- *What small step can you take to set aside time to rest mind, body, and spirit this week?*

Since marriage and singleness
are both gifts, both are
a source of God's blessing.

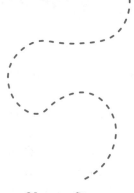

Chapter Six

Sexuality and Singleness

It was time for a coffee break, and I was hurrying down the hallway for a refill in my favorite mug. Brandon, a student whom I had just recently come to know, stopped me in my tracks to ask if I took requests for chapel programs. I explained that student suggestions are my best source for speakers and topics, and I asked what he had in mind. Brandon didn't seem to care about being overheard by others passing by when he shared his opinion emphatically that we needed a chapel series on sex—since that's what's on everybody's mind all the time.

If Brandon expected to surprise me by his suggestion, he failed. While his brashness was provocative, I took his proposal seriously and agreed with him. In fact, while the theme had not been addressed recently, it was an intentional part of our chapel curriculum to consider various dimensions of sexuality. I thanked him for sharing.

College students aren't the only ones with sex on the mind, but there is certainly a special sensitivity to issues of sexuality during the college years. It's hugely important for students to better understand their own life experiences as well as their own commitments regarding matters of sexuality.

I'm thinking of a couple of conversations that are reminders of the critical nature of life's sexual dimension. There was Paige, who I interviewed for a campus leadership position. Following an unwanted pregnancy, Paige found help from a Christian therapist in processing her complicated thoughts and feelings. But it wasn't easy.

And then there was William who had bravely posted a note on a campus bulletin board describing his struggle with same-sex attraction and inviting others with similar concerns to contact him personally. I learned from one of William's friends that the student response to his note was positive and supportive.

While stories of personal experience and the wisdom of authors, counselors, and theologians will be helpful along the way, our primary resource for this topic will be the Bible. One particular text we'll examine comes from the lips of Jesus: Matthew 19:1–12.

MANY QUESTIONS

In our discussion of sexuality, we need to clarify some terms simply and succinctly. First, with the word *sex*, we will be referring to specific acts of physical, sexual intimacy. With the word *sexuality*, we will be thinking much more broadly to include multiple dimensions of maleness and femaleness.

Sociologist Lisa McMinn explains that sexuality is a fundamental part of our humanity that involves a natural desire for relationship. In her book *Sexuality and Holy*

Longing, McMinn introduces the idea of "holy longing" to describe our human thirst for relating to others. She states that our primary longing for God (recognized or unrecognized) may be expressed in St. Augustine's famous prayer, "Our heart is restless until it rests in you."[1] But beyond a longing for God, men and women have been made with a longing for human social relationships, including the desire for sexual intimacy.[2]

When it comes to issues of sexual ethics, current conditions in today's American culture leave us with lots of questions and a great deal of confusion. What is the meaning of marriage? Is singleness a bad choice or a better choice? What are we to make of sex outside of marriage or living together? How should we understand divorce? What about same-sex attraction or marriage? The implications of these questions are vast.

It's during the critical years of college and university life that issues of sexuality are front and center—and of course, we're not just talking theory. It's all about making personal choices and setting a course for the future.

Our goal in this chapter is a modest one. Here we will simply examine an essential portion of the teaching of Jesus and seek to find personal application for twenty-first century survival.

FOUNDATIONS FOR THINKING ABOUT MARRIAGE AND SEX

Maybe any conversation about marriage is beyond your interest right now. That's fine. In the passage immediately following Matthew 19:1–9, Jesus addresses the issue of singleness. So whether you are currently married, thinking about marriage, or supposing that you will not be considering marriage anytime in the near future—it is still important for Christians to know what Jesus teaches on the subject of sexuality. Who knows how many times your personal convictions on these matters will make a difference—for yourself or someone else?

To answer our many questions about sexuality for today, we need to back up a bit. When it comes to applying biblical principles to contemporary life situations, it is encouraging to find that Jesus Himself has spoken. While the first century Pharisees were seeking to test and trap Jesus with their questions, we are able to learn from His wise response.

In Jesus' day, there was a great debate among the rabbis concerning marriage and divorce. The rabbinical controversy surrounded the interpretation of who could legally obtain a divorce. According to one school, only adultery was grounds for divorce; an opposing view held that grounds could be just about anything (as trivial as burnt toast).[3] So the debate raged on, and the Jewish community was divided.

> **Some Pharisees came to him [Jesus] to test him. They asked, "Is it lawful for a man to divorce his wife for any and every reason?"**
>
> **"Haven't you read," he replied, "that at the beginning the Creator 'made them male and female,' and said, 'For this reason a man will leave his father and mother and be united to his wife, and the two will become one flesh'? So they are no longer two, but one flesh. Therefore what God has joined together, let no one separate."**

> **"Why then," they asked, "did Moses command that a man give his wife a certificate of divorce and send her away?"**
>
> **Jesus replied, "Moses permitted you to divorce your wives because your hearts were hard. But it was not this way from the beginning. I tell you that anyone who divorces his wife, except for sexual immorality, and marries another woman commits adultery."** (Matt. 19:3–9)

When Jesus points his listeners to the Genesis account of creation, He is describing the world prior to the entrance of sin. Jesus avoids the Pharisees' trap regarding divorce in order to emphasize God's original design for marriage.

First and foremost, Jesus is saying we need to recognize what God intended in marriage: a man and a woman united together, becoming one flesh. Here, Jesus is quoting Genesis 2:24, "That is why a man leaves his father and mother and is united to his wife, and they become one flesh." Then Jesus adds His personal commentary that this one-flesh marriage relationship is God's doing—"what God has joined together." Furthermore, Jesus says that this divine joining of a man and a woman must not be undone—"let no one separate."

Well, the Pharisees are listening, but they aren't understanding. They're still intent on getting Jesus to comment on divorce. So they ask again, "Why then . . . did Moses command that a man give his wife a certificate of divorce and send her away?" With great patience, Jesus explains.

In His response, Jesus allows that sexual immorality is indeed legitimate grounds for divorce—but again, He pushes our thinking back to the beginning, back to God's intention for marriage—that originally, "it was not this way" (Matt. 19:8). Allowance for divorce comes only because sin has entered the world—and people's hearts became hard. But there's a better way.

We can conclude that Jesus has a high view of marriage— as a covenantal relationship between a man and a woman.[4] Jesus' quotation of Genesis 2:24 contains more than we may have seen at first glance. Note the sequence: leaving father and mother comes first, then being united together in covenantal marriage, and finally becoming one flesh (including sexual intimacy).

As Jesus quotes Genesis 2:24, He is affirming the authoritative teaching of Scripture. Implicit in these words from Genesis and Matthew are the following:

- That marriage—by God's design—is between a man and a woman
- That a covenantal commitment unites a couple in a life-long partnership
- That sexual intimacy is a privilege of the marriage relationship

With these biblical principles in mind, pastor and theologian Tim Keller describes the divinely prescribed place of sex in marriage this way: "Sex is God's appointed way for two people to reciprocally say to one another, 'I belong completely, permanently, and exclusively to you.'"[5] Not exactly a casual sex philosophy.

We can also conclude from Matthew 19 that Jesus has a high view of sex. Not only do we see that the one-flesh relationship of sex exists within the confines of the marriage covenant, but we also see that sex outside of the marriage covenant is such a serious violation of marriage that it is grounds for severing the covenant.

Finally, it's significant to note that while sexual immorality is legitimate grounds for divorce, such a violation does not *require* divorce. Forgiveness with reconciliation may be a biblical option (see Matt. 18:15). In any case, Christ-following couples experiencing even the most stressful of marital conflicts are always required to extend and receive forgiveness.

WHAT ABOUT PREMARITAL SEX?

According to recent estimates of the US Census Bureau, the median age at which men and women marry for the first time in the United States is higher than ever, with women entering their first marriage at 27.8 years and men at 29.8 years.[6]

Of course, this means that most college and university students are unmarried. As we consider these demographics, it is important to remember that the common practice of couples living together prior to marriage has elevated the ages for first marriages. The director of a relatively recent research study concluded, "Premarital sex is normal behavior for the vast majority of Americans, and has been for decades."[7]

An article in *The Atlantic* entitled, "The Sex Recession," documents that young people are becoming sexually active later now than in previous generations. Studies have found that from 1991 to 2017, high school students having sexual intercourse dropped from 54% to 40%. While this seems to be an encouraging trend, the opening statement of the article is more troubling: "The share of Americans who say sex between unmarried adults is 'not wrong at all' is at an all time high."[8]

In the face of these statistics, it seems old-fashioned if not impossible to insist that sexual intimacy should be reserved for marriage. For a young man or woman to claim virginity or that they are waiting to be married before engaging in sex is a surefire way to elicit a disapproving frown, sympathetic smile, or full-blown laughter. And the talk behind one's back is even worse. Who likes being called a puritanical prude?

If ever there were an ethic outside of the current cultural norm, it's this one—God's teaching that sexual intimacy is intended for marriage and *only* for marriage. But this is what the Bible teaches, and as Christians, we simply cannot avoid it.

At the age of thirty, Lauren Winner (now on the faculty at Duke Divinity School) wrote a book especially helpful for Christian singles—*Real Sex: The Naked Truth about Chastity*. Here's how she describes her personal struggle with Christian sexual ethics:

> For several years, I tried and tried to find a way to wiggle out of the church's traditional teaching that God requires chastity outside of marriage, and I failed. I read all the classics of 1970s Christian sexual ethics, all appealing and comforting books that insisted that Christians must avoid not sex outside of marriage, but rather exploitative sex, or sex where you run the risk of getting hurt. . . . But in the end, I was never able to square sex outside of marriage with the Christian story about God, redemption, and human bodies.[9]

Does this mean that the Bible is against sex? Not at all. The Bible is for sex. Sex within marriage is part of God's good and beautiful design for the welfare and happiness of humankind. Not only does the Bible acknowledge the procreative purpose of sex (Gen. 1:28), but Scripture is not embarrassed to speak of sexual pleasure in marriage. The Old Testament book of the Song of Solomon is explicit in its poetic description of the physical dimension of marital love.

Still, there are biblical boundaries associated with sex. It's the seventh commandment that tells us: "You shall not commit adultery" (Ex. 20:14). We might say this commandment *implicitly* forbids all sexual relations outside of biblical marriage, including premarital sex (sometimes called fornication).

An *explicit* biblical text prohibiting all extramarital sexual relations is 1 Corinthians 6:18. The English term *sexual immorality* translates the Greek word *porneia*, which has a broad and inclusive meaning referring to any form of sexual intercourse outside of heterosexual marriage.[10] Sex outside of the bond of marriage is a violation of God's will. The apostle Paul urges his readers:

> **Flee from sexual immorality. All other sins a person commits are outside the body, but whoever sins sexually, sins against their own body. Do you not know that your bodies are temples of the Holy Spirit, who is in you, whom you have received from God? You are not your own; you were bought at a price. Therefore honor God with your bodies.** (1 Cor. 6:18–20)

BUT WHY?

Hopefully, you would agree that the biblical teaching on sex and marriage is clear and straightforward—sex is intended for marriage between a man and a woman.

But why? Maybe you're thinking that the only answer is, "Because God said so." Yes, God said so. But *why* did God say so?

The biblical sex ethic is more than just a set of rules. As we read the Scriptures, breathed out by God, we find more than isolated commands and artificial restrictions. God's love letter to humanity is gospel—it's good news intended for human fulfillment and flourishing. When God created us as male and female with bodies and pronounced His creation as "very good," we can be assured that there was purpose behind that design. When God describes the marriage relationship as a one-flesh relationship, we can conclude that there is purpose behind that picture—for our good.

It doesn't take much imagination to conclude that the biblical term "one flesh" (Gen. 2:24) refers to sexual intercourse. But even more than that, it includes an emotional and spiritual unity intended for marriage. Lauren Winner, in her book *Real Sex* puts it this way:

> When it comes to sex, one cannot leave out marriage. The *no* to sex outside marriage seems arbitrary and cruel apart from the Creator's *yes* to sex within marriage. Indeed, one can say that in Christianity's vocabulary the only real sex is the sex that happens in a marriage; the faux sex that goes on outside marriage is not really sex at all. The physical coming together that happens between two people who are not married is only a distorted imitation of sex.[11]

So, why is sex for marriage only? It's because God created sex for marriage, for our good—where a man and a woman give to each other—body, mind, and soul. And that's real sex.

Before leaving this subject, pause and reflect on your own life experience. This biblical truth may be exposing hurt, guilt, and shame because of personal failure. It could be that more than anything else you need to embrace the love of God and the healing that comes with confession and repentance. The Scripture reminds us, "If we confess our sins to God, he can always be trusted to forgive us and take our sins away" (1 John 1:9 CEV).

Our Lord wants to give us a fresh start as we walk in His loving grace. The Bible is all about "second chances" (or more—on and on). No matter where we have been or what we have done, we need not continue thinking that it's too late to change. It's never too late to acknowledge our need and to reach out to Jesus. Our culture prescribes one path to happiness. It's in every sitcom and every movie, but it's a lie, and it will disappoint. Jesus prescribes another path, a path worth following for good reason. Jesus knows us and loves us even more than we love ourselves. We can trust Him to show us the way.

WHAT JESUS SAYS ABOUT SINGLENESS

Let's continue our study of Jesus' teaching in Matthew 19. Once Jesus has clarified God's design for marriage based on Genesis 2:24, and after He showed His hand on the issue of divorce—allowable in cases of sexual immorality—His disciples are wondering if marriage is for them.

Remember, in that culture, marriages were arranged by parents,[12] and if results were unsatisfactory, maybe singleness is the better way to go—at least, that's what the disciples were thinking. Here's how the conversation went:

> **The disciples said to him, "If this is the situation between a husband and wife, it is better not to marry."**
>
> **Jesus replied, "Not everyone can accept this word, but only those to whom it has been given. For there are eunuchs who were born that way, and there are eunuchs who have been made eunuchs by others—and there are those who choose to live like eunuchs for the sake of the kingdom of heaven. The one who can accept this should accept it." (Matt. 19:10–12)**

Sure enough, Jesus sympathizes with the disciples. Yes, indeed, it may be better not to marry, but "not everyone can accept this word."[13] Jesus goes on to explain how it may be possible for the single life to be one's best choice. Jesus is using the word "eunuch" metaphorically to speak of men who are impotent by birth, by circumstance, or by choice. The eunuch would be a person who is single and celibate. And, according to Jesus, the one who can accept this should accept it.

It's worth observing that the founder of the Christian faith (Jesus) along with the chief theologian of the Christian faith (the apostle Paul) were both single men. While it's certainly true that throughout the Bible there are affirmations of family life and sexual intimacy, it is also true that the Bible allows for and affirms the choice of singleness. As we have seen, this single life would be a celibate life. Again, while the Bible endorses and celebrates sex within marriage, the Bible also presents the celibate state as a special opportunity for faithful service in the kingdom of God.

Not only were the Lord Jesus and the apostle Paul single themselves, but the Scriptures record the teaching of both of them regarding the single life. This revolutionary affirmation of singleness in adulthood distinguished Christianity from Judaism and other religions in the first century.[14] Here in Matthew 19:11–12, Jesus is saying in essence that singleness may be a calling of God for the sake of the kingdom of God. In such a vocation, disciples are following their Lord in ministry and embracing a celibate life. The apostle Paul says virtually the same thing in 1 Corinthians 7:7 when he refers to his own singleness and the call to celibacy as a divine gift: "I wish that all of you were as I am. But each of you has your own gift from God; one has this gift, another has that." Paul concludes that the single life allows for a focus on ministry and freedom from family concerns (see 1 Cor. 7:32–35).

The clear inference from the teaching of Jesus in Matthew 19 and Paul in 1 Corinthians 7 is that the married life or the single life are both legitimate callings for the believer. Since marriage and singleness are both gifts, both are a source of God's blessing.

Pastor and theologian John Piper has crafted a sermon that speaks especially to singles, but finds application to marrieds as well. His sermon closes with these powerful points:

- "That the family of God grows not by propagation through sexual intercourse, but by regeneration through faith in Christ;

- That relationships in Christ are more permanent, and more precious, than relationships in families;
- That marriage is temporary, and finally gives way to the relationship to which it was pointing all along: Christ and the church—the way a picture is no longer needed when you see face to face;
- And that faithfulness to Christ defines the value of life; all other relationships get their final significance from this. No family relationship is ultimate; relationship to Christ is."[15]

SAME-SEX SEXUAL RELATIONSHIPS AND THE BIBLE

There is a relatively small number of biblical texts that deal specifically with the issue of what we might generally call same-sex sexual behavior (see endnote for texts).[16] But that small number does not automatically mean that same-sex sexual relationships are not a concern of the Bible or that it is not an important issue.

Jesus never once mentions same-sex sexual relationships. However, we need not conclude that the issue was unimportant to Jesus. As we have seen, Jesus does speak to the subject of marriage, and this has implications for individuals who experience attraction to the same sex since Jesus viewed marriage as a union between a man and a woman.

The limited amount of biblical material may simply mean that the Jewish and Christian positions on these matters were quite clear and well-known. A plain reading of the Old and New Testaments leads to the conclusion that same-sex sexual behavior is outside of the will of God.

Moreover, there are no biblical texts that affirm, endorse, or encourage same-sex sexual relationships. For generations, the church around the world has been consistent in its teaching on homosexuality.[17]

In our consideration of sexual identity, it is important to draw a distinction between same-sex attraction and same-sex sexual behavior. Christians may struggle for a lifetime with same-sex attraction without acting on those desires in same-sex sexual practice. Of course, the believer's fight with temptation and pursuit of holiness are present in any area of struggle. Since a biblical view of marriage limits sexual intimacy to a married man and woman, the biblical standard for singleness is celibacy.

Wesley Hill authored *Washed and Waiting: Reflections on Christian Faithfulness and Homosexuality*.[18] From the time he was in high school, Wesley struggled with feelings of same-sex attraction. As a follower of Jesus, Wesley consistently sought to live faithfully to Scripture in obedience to the Lord. He understood the sinfulness of same-sex sexual relations, and he maintained a celibate life. His wrestling with brokenness and loneliness continued through high school, college, and beyond. Through prayer and the counsel of wise believers, Wesley sought help and healing in every dimension of his life.

Wesley came to describe his life as "washed and waiting." As a Christian, his embrace of Christ as Lord and Savior meant that he was "washed"—forgiven and saved. He was a believer on the path of following Jesus in the process of sanctification through Christian disciplines and the fellowship of the church. While Wesley's same-sex sexual feelings remained, he learned to be content in a celibate life of faithfulness to the Lord and "waiting" for the time when God makes all things new—not in this life but the next.

Rosaria Champagne Butterfield, author of *The Secret Thoughts of an Unlikely Convert: An English Professor's Journey into Christian Faith*,[19] was living an enjoyable and fulfilling life as a tenured professor of English at Syracuse University. Teaching Gay and Lesbian Studies along with Queer Theory was consistent with her secular, feminist worldview and personal life in a relationship with another woman.

Then the unexpected happened. Through the gracious hospitality of an area pastor and his wife, Rosaria came to understand and then embrace the gospel of Jesus Christ. Her conversion to the Christian faith was so dramatic that Rosaria compares it to a train wreck. Her previous opinion of Christianity was harsh and condemning. Ultimately, Rosaria left her professorship at Syracuse and broke up with her lesbian partner. She has since married a pastor in North Carolina where Rosaria is a homeschool mother, author, and speaker.

Rosaria's convictions about Christianity and sexuality have changed completely since her days as a professor in New York. Here's what she writes in her book, *Openness Unhindered*:

> Bible-believing Christians are gender and sexuality essentialists, believing that there is an essence to maleness and femaleness, and that God's created order mandates sexual union exclusively between one man and one woman in the covenant of biblical marriage.[20]

As we seek to understand and faithfully apply biblical principles regarding sexuality, we can confidently conclude that God's best for men and women is celibacy in single-ness or fidelity in the covenant of marriage between a man and a woman. God may not take away a person's same-sex attraction, but He certainly has the ability to do that. In any case, all who follow Jesus have temptations and struggles that require the ongoing empowerment of the Holy Spirit and a significant measure of God's grace.

CARING FOR FRIENDS

So how should we interact with our friends who are liv-ing contrary to Jesus' teaching on sexuality? With sincere love and compassion, we must affirm the worth and value of all people since every person is created in God's image and loved by our Creator. With true care and humility, we must acknowledge that all people suffer with weakness and brokenness, and every person is in need of growing into greater conformity with the life and teaching of Jesus. And then, our conversation must be governed by these essential principles: helping others gently (Gal. 6:1); "speaking the truth in love" (Eph. 4:15); and caring without a judgmental attitude (Matt. 7:1–6).

WHERE'S YOUR ID?

Who are you? Your response to that inquiry may largely depend on who's asking the question. An initial response might be to simply provide your name. But maybe the ques-tioner is looking for something else—your school, year in school, major, team, organization, position, or your occupation. If you had just been stopped by a police officer, you can assume that the question of identity would be answered best by providing a drivers license and registration. In some circumstances, you might even answer questions of identity in sexual or relational terms. Man or woman, married or single.

So who are you? Beyond all the labels, there is a more substantive way of describing our identity—a better, deeper, truer way of claiming identity. When we embrace the gospel of Christ and find forgiveness for all of our failures, we can claim an identity in Christ as a follower of Jesus. As the apostle Paul concludes a discussion of sexuality in his first letter to the Corinthians, he offers this word regarding Christian identity: "Whoever is united with the Lord is one with him in spirit" (1 Cor. 6:17).

May God help us to experience our sexuality according to His plan and purpose. May God give us the grace to trust Him as we find all that we are meant to be in Christ.

A Step Further

- *What is God's view of marriage?*

- *What is our culture's view of marriage?*

- *How does God's view and our culture's view of same-sex sexual relationships differ?*

- *How should a Christ follower interact with people who live contrary to biblical teaching on sexuality?*

- *Is it possible to be gay and a Christian?*

- *Am I willing to be single and celibate?*

- *Am I courageous enough to wait, from this day on, for sex within the bounds of marriage?*

The teaching of Jesus on
servanthood is an antidote
to the empty, hollow,
lonely life of me-ism.

Chapter Seven

Beyond Me-ism—Servanthood

It was the last week of Jesus' earthly life. His three-year ministry of teaching, healing, and announcing the coming kingdom was drawing to a close. Jesus was just hours away from facing the most excruciating suffering imaginable in a brutal crucifixion. And beyond the visible pain of a tortuous execution, there was the invisible pain of bearing the penalty for human sin. No one can come close to imagining the anguish that Jesus faced.

Yet, on that evening just prior to those horrific events leading to Golgotha, Jesus met with His disciples for a meal and instruction that they could never have predicted. In a private room around a table, Jesus teaches His friends one more lesson on the nature of love. No one could bring this lesson more powerfully than Jesus: the love of God is a love that serves.

It was a simple, ordinary yet utterly profound act when Jesus got up from the table, wrapped a towel around His waist, and washed the feet of His disciples. He displayed love brilliantly—a sacrificial love, with passion for others, a servant love. By His example, Jesus is teaching us that servanthood is love in action.

In that final meeting with his disciples, when Jesus had so much in His heart and mind, our Lord uses precious moments to teach a lesson He had modeled on a daily basis over the years—a lesson in servanthood (John 13:1–17).

The "me-ism" of our twenty-first century American culture underscores our need to heed the voice of Jesus. Egotism defined by an obsession with self and lack of concern for others is all too common. The teaching of Jesus on servanthood is an antidote to the empty, hollow, lonely life of me-ism.

THE PARABLE OF THE GOOD SAMARITAN

From beginning to end, the life and teaching of Jesus emphasizes and exemplifies the theme of servant love. In the parable of the Good Samaritan where Jesus identifies the meaning of "neighbor," he teaches the importance of loving our neighbor and explains the radical nature of love that serves.

Christian or not, most people know what a Good Samaritan is. English dictionaries commonly define a Good Samaritan as "a charitable or helpful person." Think of the number of hospitals that are named Good Samaritan. Nearly two thousand years after Jesus told His parable, people are still talking about Good Samaritans. I don't know of a more important time in human history for us to give attention to the teaching of Jesus in this familiar parable.

In Luke 10:25–37 the Scripture says:

On one occasion an expert in the law stood up to test Jesus. "Teacher," he asked, "what must I do to inherit eternal life?"

"What is written in the Law?" he replied. "How do you read it?"

He answered, "'Love the Lord your God with all your heart and with all your soul and with all your strength and with all your mind'; and, 'Love your neighbor as yourself.'"

"You have answered correctly," Jesus replied. "Do this and you will live."

But he wanted to justify himself, so he asked Jesus, "And who is my neighbor?"

In reply Jesus said: "A man was going down from Jerusalem to Jericho, when he was attacked by robbers. They stripped him of his clothes, beat him and went away, leaving him half dead. A priest happened to be going down the same road, and when he saw the man, he passed by on the other side. So too, a Levite, when he came to the place and saw him, passed by on the other side. But a Samaritan, as he traveled, came where the man was; and when he saw him, he took pity on him. He went to him and bandaged his wounds, pouring on oil and wine. Then he put the man on his own donkey, brought him to an inn and took care of him. The next day he took out two denarii and gave them to the innkeeper. 'Look after him,' he said, 'and when I return, I will reimburse you for any extra expense you may have.'

"Which of these three do you think was a neighbor to the man who fell into the hands of robbers?"

The expert in the law replied, "The one who had mercy on him."

Jesus told him, "Go and do likewise."

In the narrative that leads to the parable itself, "an expert in the law,"—a lawyer and religious scholar well-versed in Jewish law—came to Jesus with two questions. It's hard to know how sincere this man was with his concern about eternal life and his wondering about the meaning of neighbor. Luke says that he came to "test Jesus" (v. 25) and to "justify himself" (v. 29).

The Jews of Jesus' day lived in what we might call a gated community, where membership was carefully restricted. For the first-century Jew, "neighbor" simply meant "fellow-Jew"—a narrow interpretation of Torah that actually denied the real intention of God's law.[1]

The lawyer's attempt at self-justification came with the question, "Who is my neighbor?" He was saying, "What's the big deal? Okay, I do this. I love my Jewish neighbor!" But—surprise, surprise! Jesus' definition of neighbor is beyond anything the lawyer could imagine.

This parable that Jesus tells could have been based on a real-life event. The details make it sound like a historical incident. In fact, over the centuries, assaults and robberies have occurred regularly on the Jericho Road—a 17-mile stretch that had come to be known as "The Red, or Bloody, Way."[2] While the traveler who is beaten is identified simply as "a man" (v. 30), it is a clear assumption that this man is a Jew.[3]

Of all the players in this parable—including the robbers, the man who is beaten, the priest who passes by, the Levite who does the same, and the innkeeper who receives the injured man—it's the Samaritan who takes center stage.

Identifying this helper as a Samaritan is what makes the parable so powerful.

In those days, a Samaritan was someone from Samaria, a region where people were racially and spiritually mixed— part Jewish and part Gentile. Because of that mixture, Jews hated Samaritans, and Samaritans returned the favor. Their history went way back, and reprehensible behavior came from both sides.

The level of animosity between Jews and the Samaritans can be seen right here in Jesus' encounter with the lawyer. Once Jesus completes his parable—applauding the conduct of the Samaritan and defining a neighbor as anyone in need—Jesus asks the lawyer, "Which of these three do you think was a neighbor to the man who fell into the hands of robbers?" How does the lawyer respond? He says, "The one who had mercy on him." With such deep-seated aversion to this people-group, the lawyer can't even bring himself to pronounce the word Samaritan.[4]

When Jesus makes the Samaritan the hero of his story, we can see that he's not out to win friends and influence people among the Jewish population. While it's true that the story Jesus tells could have come right out of Israel's daily news, a typical reporting of the facts may have revealed that the robbers were Samaritans![5] So when Jesus teaches about loving neighbors and tells a story where a Samaritan is the good guy, he's teaching something new and unexpected. Jesus is agitating his Jewish audience.

This is what the parables of Jesus often do—they agitate us. Do you know what they call the little steel ball in a spray-paint can? It's called an agitator. What's it for? It's to stir things up. And that's what Jesus' parables do. They shake things up—and they challenge us to think in new ways. This is why parables are so intriguing and important. As hard-hitting and unpredictable agitators, Jesus' stories disturb our comfort zone.

THE LEAST WE CAN DO

We have an on-going joke in our family. If I happen to do a good deed for my wife or son, I'll follow-up by saying, "Well, it's the least that I can do, and you know that I always want to do the least." I'd like to apply that phrase to the lawyer here in Luke 10. When the man asked Jesus to define the meaning of neighbor, I believe he was looking for a way out. The religious scholar was looking to justify his own prejudice and behavior. He was looking to do the very minimum—the very least that he had to do.[6]

College professors are usually quite put-off by students who raise a particular question in the classroom. It's that profound inquiry probing the content of a scintillating lecture: "Is that going to be on the exam?" In other words, the student is saying, "Let me know the very least that I have to do."

The lawyer wanted to do the very least. He wanted to love only his friends. What a hard teaching it was for the lawyer to hear this parable. How difficult it must have been for this upstanding religious leader to be given a lesson in morality based on the meritorious action of a Samaritan. The lesson of Jesus' parable is unambiguous: loving your neighbor means much more than loving your friend or like-minded acquaintance.

WHO IS OUR NEIGHBOR?

So then, just who is our neighbor? It's the person in the ditch needing our help; the one who may never pay us back; the one who may be unable or unwilling to express thanks.[7] Our job is not to investigate how the person may have fallen into the ditch or to condemn someone who has made foolish decisions that led to their lying in the ditch. Our responsibility is to help the person out of the ditch.

While the teaching of this parable is to encourage "neighbor love" and to define a neighbor as one who is in need, there is also a clear and powerful subtext: love of neighbor must transcend religion, race, ethnicity, and any other human difference. It's a brief and simple parable. We know the content well. But the applications are broad and the implications are stretching.

Too often, the parable of the Good Samaritan is considered simply (and simplistically) to be a call to help people in need. Jesus is teaching us more. And maybe the most critical teaching of this parable involves the scope of our call. Jesus' parable is teaching that loving God and loving your neighbor means loving the whole world. You might say that more than anything, Jesus is teaching about the universal neighborhood of God.[8]

Yes, Jesus is answering the lawyer's question, "Who is my neighbor?" But Bible scholar David Garland astutely observes that there is a false assumption in that question, "Who is my neighbor?" The false assumption is that "there is such a thing as a non-neighbor; the parable says there is no such person."[9] Every human being is our neighbor, created in the image of God and worthy of being loved.

LOVING ENEMIES—REALLY?

You may recall that in our study of perfectionism in chapter three, we looked at the words of Jesus in the Sermon on the Mount: "Be perfect, therefore, as your heavenly Father is perfect" (Matt. 5:48). In the context, just four verses earlier, Jesus said, "Love your enemies and pray for those who persecute you" (Matt. 5:44). In calling us to "be perfect," Jesus is challenging us to emulate the all-embracing perfect love of our heavenly Father, so far as to love even our enemies.

In Jesus' parable the Samaritan and the Jew were functionally enemies. Their nationalities and religious practices were different, and there was a deep-seated animosity between the two groups. Yet, the Samaritan loved the Jew in distress.

From an Atlanta jail cell, Martin Luther King Jr. wrote a sermon entitled "Loving Your Enemies." Dr. King challenges us with these profound and powerful words:

> Returning hate for hate multiplies hate, adding deeper darkness to a night already devoid of stars. . . . Hate brings irreparable damage to its victims. . . . Hate is just as injurious to the person who hates. . . . Love is the only force capable of transforming an enemy into a friend.[10]

Issues of race and ethnicity are woven into Jesus' teaching. Communities can be drawn together as its members practice care and compassion across racial and ethnic differences and other differences as well.

Daniel was a Korean-American college student just completing his junior year. It was Daniel's third year as a member of the Asian Student Fellowship (ASF) on campus, and he enjoyed the friendships within that fellowship over the years. For him, ASF was a place where he could be himself.

In conversation with Daniel one afternoon, I asked: "How do members of a minority culture see themselves?" And then, "How do minority students relate to each other and to those outside of their own culture?" Daniel confessed that ethnic differences often lead to conflict and misunderstanding where people aren't considerate of each other, marginalize others, and aren't hospitable to one another.

Daniel was especially encouraged by the leadership of the ASF that had set the goal of making the entire campus a safer place for every student. Specifically, students were challenging each other to consider what it would mean to walk in the shoes of someone of a different ethnicity— empathizing with another person's experience.

GLOBAL AND INDIVIDUAL APPLICATIONS

This teaching of Jesus has applications on the global level as well as the individual level. Here is a call to neighbor love that extends to a global interest in reaching out to needy people around the world whoever they are and wherever they may be. When natural disasters and other catastrophes strike people in distant lands, the opportunity is there for Christ followers to reach out to the grieving and suffering. We are following Jesus by administering aid, offering relief, and sharing resources with those in need—regardless of religion, race, ethnicity, or any other distinction.

It's a call to individuals to reach out beyond personal

concerns and private interests; and it's a call for wealthy nations to act with compassion for the hungry, the hurting, and the homeless in the poorest parts of our world.[11]

In this parable of the Good Samaritan, Jesus is inviting us to participate with Him in the building of a kingdom that is countercultural. It's a kingdom that gives attention to the marginalized. It's a kingdom that is quite different from what we may be used to. It's a kingdom of *real* compassion that requires *real* activity that will have *real* costs.

Henri Nouwen, Donald McNeill, and Douglas Morrison are the authors of a little book entitled *Compassion: A Reflection on the Christian Life*. Here's how these authors define and describe Christian compassion: "The word *compassion* is derived from the Latin words *pati* and *cum*, which together mean 'to suffer with.'"[12] The authors go on to say:

> Compassion requires us to be weak with the weak,
> vulnerable with the vulnerable, and powerless with the
> powerless. Compassion means full immersion in the
> condition of being human.[13]

Jesus never minimized the cost of servanthood. It's no wonder that the longer Jesus preached, the more opposition He received. His teaching was radical, and the implications were clear to the lawyer who heard it first and to all who have heard it since. Jesus was saying, "Go and do likewise" (v. 37). Jesus was insisting that our love and care for people must go beyond our circle of friends, beyond the easy and the comfortable, beyond the borders and barriers that keep people apart.

LIVING WITH HUMILITY—SERVANTHOOD

But how, then, do we live with such love and care for people—and with the humility of servanthood? Of course, we're asking the wrong question if we're looking for a formula. Servanthood is motivated by a heart of humility; servanthood is love in action—modeled most brilliantly by Jesus who said of Himself, "The Son of Man did not come to be served, but to serve" (Matt. 20:28).

The apostle Paul urges us to follow Jesus' humble servanthood:

> **In your relationships with one another, have the same mindset as Christ Jesus: Who, being in very nature God, did not consider equality with God something to be used to his own advantage; rather, he made himself nothing by taking the very nature of a servant, being made in human likeness. And being found in appearance as a man, he humbled himself by becoming obedient to death—even death on a cross!**
> (Phil. 2:5–8)

What are the more personal dimensions of living out the teaching of the parable of the Good Samaritan in daily life? Jesus' lesson challenges us when we fail to extend common courtesy to everyone, when those in the majority culture treat with contempt those of a minority culture, and when friendships are so tight and secure that welcoming others never happens. It may be scary and uncomfortable to cross invisible barriers we have constructed, but being a faithful follower of Jesus requires us to offer a listening ear, to extend a helping hand, to act with genuine care. You don't have to agree with people to show love to them. You don't have to be exactly like others to engage them. You don't have to compromise your personal convictions and your deeply held faith to reach out to a neighbor in need.

Pastor and psychologist Dr. Siang-Yang Tan offers some simple and positive, everyday suggestions for putting into practice the virtues of humility and servanthood. Here's a short list:

- Be on time for appointments
- Keep your commitments and promises
- Bring food to a sick neighbor
- Send a card of appreciation or affirmation
- Let people know that you noticed their kindness, encouragement, or listening.[14]

Dr. Tan quotes the seventeenth-century Christian author Jeremy Taylor who writes: "Nurture a love to do good things in secret, concealed from the eyes of others and therefore not highly esteemed because of them. Be content to go without praise."[15] Wow—a tough assignment for all of us struggling with the "me-ism" syndrome!

BEYOND ME-ISM

Our twenty-first century American culture is far more about pride and arrogance than humility and service. In our human nature, we tend to focus on ourselves and what we want others to see of us. The teaching of Jesus by word and example calls us to a life beyond me-ism.

We all need a biblical reminder of our Lord's priority

of servanthood. Applications of Jesus' parable abound, and opportunities for loving our neigbor are in front of us all day long. In a world of suffering and need, we are faced with this question: What can we do? The lawyer challenging Jesus was concerned about "doing the least that he could do." May God help us—not to do the least we can do, but so much more—for Christ's kingdom and for the good of everyone around us.

Theologian and author Richard Foster offers this encouragement:

> The risen Christ beckons us to the ministry of the towel. Perhaps you would like to begin by experimenting with a prayer that a number of us have used. Begin the day by praying, "Lord Jesus, I would so appreciate it if You would bring me someone today whom I can serve."[16]

A Step Further

- *Read the story of the Good Samaritan three times slowly. What is one thing that you see now that you had not seen before?*

- *Can you think of a time that someone has treated you with cruelty? How did you feel?*

- *Who is your neighbor?*

- *Describe an experience where someone has come alongside you as a neighbor.*

- *Have you ever sensed God calling you to help someone and you didn't take the opportunity?*

- *What do you have in abundance that you could share with others—time, money, knowledge, a listening ear, physical strength?*

As relational human beings,
God uses Christian community for
our spiritual and emotional
well-being and ultimate good.

Chapter Eight

Living in a Safe Place—Community

Bethany was an enthusiastic college freshman. After about a month on campus, she was growing accustomed to the new freedoms of college life and the challenges of keeping up with demanding course assignments. From all outward appearances, Bethany was adjusting quite well to her new environment in every way, except for one. Bethany confessed to me that she was extremely lonely and she planned to fly home for fall break.

Bethany's story fits the profile of what I have witnessed quite commonly among first-year students. Citing the results of a survey by the American College Health Association, *New York Times* op-ed columnist Frank Bruni writes about college loneliness in an article entitled, "The Real Campus Scourge."[1]

In Bethany's case, she did, indeed, fly home for fall break. But spring break was spent at the home of a college friend, and her summer as a camp counselor demonstrated some healthy emotional growth. Bethany was finding friends and developing new relationships as she reached out to others. Simple things like keeping an open door in her dorm and participating in floor events made a difference. But even this took initiative. Bethany learned that entering into friendships does not happen automatically.

HOW IMPORTANT ARE FRIENDS?

In my college chaplaincy, I conducted exit interviews of about two dozen graduating seniors every spring. One of the key questions I asked was this: "What are some of the most positive influences on your spiritual life during your college years?" The most cited response: friends. Students would say that relationships were the key part of their college experience. And why were friends so important? The answers went like this: "They challenge me; they love me; they empathize with me; they encourage me."

Zach, a graduating senior, explained that the discipleship small group he joined with five other guys during his freshman year was especially formative. The regularity of their meeting was a constant source of support. Zach acknowledged his great appreciation for this group in saying that he couldn't have made it through his four years of college without these friends.

While a college or university campus may be buzzing with activity—crowded lecture halls, active dormitories, and busy athletic facilities—an individual student can get lost in the middle of it all. In order to combat loneliness, college administration and students themselves need to take the initiative in making the college environment a community experience. Residence hall programs, student development activities, intramural sports options, and even extracurricular academic functions can connect students who would otherwise struggle alone.

Of course, loneliness isn't limited to college freshmen, but extends to all who lack friendship and community. C. S. Lewis helps us bridge the fear and hesitation that may be sustaining our feelings of loneliness. He explains that sharing common interests, insights, or even burdens may be a first step in finding a friend. Lewis puts it this way: "The typical expression of opening friendship would be something like, 'What? You too? I thought I was the only one.'"[2]

What is community? How can we define it? Will Willimon and Tom Naylor in their book on "Rethinking Higher Education" define community as "a partnership of people committed to the care and nurturing of each other's mind, body, heart, and soul."[3]

People need community. It's important in the college environment because college prepares one for life. Habits developed during the college years can set critical patterns. What we learn in college—outside the classroom as well as inside the classroom—can make all the difference in the world for our intellectual, physical, spiritual, and emotional well-being.

I have a personal illustration of the value of community through my experience with motorcycling. This interest in biking goes way back to the influence that came from my father as a motorcycle cop. Over the years, I have owned and ridden a number of Harley-Davidsons.

The motorcycling community is a fraternity of sorts. On the highway, passing bikers connect with a casual wave. The bond between motorcyclists is revealed even more clearly when the bikes are parked and conversation is shared—beginning easily with observations about bikes, weather, road conditions, or the joy of riding. There is a rider connection here, a community, an understanding among motorcyclists that if you arc in nccd or in troublc, a biker buddy will be there to help.

CHRISTIAN COMMUNITY DEFINED

German pastor and theologian Dietrich Bonhoeffer helps us understand the distinctive nature of Christian community in his book *Life Together*. Bonhoeffer compellingly describes the connectedness that exists between believers as he defines Christian community this way:

> Christianity means community through Jesus Christ and in Jesus Christ. No Christian community is more or less than this. Whether it be a brief, single encounter or the daily fellowship of years, **Christian community is only this. We belong to one another only through and in Jesus Christ.**[4] (emphasis added)

There are all kinds of communities in this world because it's consistent with our human nature to gravitate toward community. But there is a uniqueness in Christian community. Christ followers—wherever they are—have a special connectedness to other Christ followers. Christians are not just random, isolated individuals. Believers in Jesus have a common need for each other and a distinctive purpose together for the advance of Christ's kingdom.

One of many brilliant biblical descriptions of God's people living in community is found in the apostle Paul's letter to the Colossians:

Therefore, as God's chosen people, holy and dearly loved, clothe yourselves with compassion, kindness, humility, gentleness and patience. Bear with each other and forgive one another if any of you has a grievance against someone. Forgive as the Lord forgave you. And over all these virtues put on love, which binds them all together in perfect unity.
(Col. 3:12–14)

This is our starting point in comprehending God's design for Christian community as we understand that as a chosen people, we are part of something that is far bigger than ourselves as individuals. We are part of a whole line of people that goes back to the New Testament church and Old Testament Israel. Together, we are related to those of every era who have been the recipients of the special grace of God's love through Jesus.

It's like sitting in the stands at a college or university football stadium. We're not alone on those bleachers as we are surrounded by a crowd with rows and rows of fans. In the stadium of Christian community, we can be thankful to God that we have been given a ticket to the game. We're sitting with our friends—related to each other, in need of each other, and thriving in relationship with each other.

Here we are. This is it. The big idea of this chapter—as relational human beings, God uses Christian community for our spiritual and emotional well-being and ultimate good.

CHRISTIAN COMMUNITY:
BIBLICALLY EXPANDED

We can amplify this biblical description of Christian community by backing up one verse in our Colossians text. "Here there is no Gentile or Jew, circumcised or uncircumcised, barbarian, Scythian, slave or free, but Christ is all, and is in all" (Col. 3:11).

This distinctively Christian community is distinctively diverse. As we saw in Chapter 7 with the parable of the Good Samaritan, Christ breaks down all barriers. For Christians living in community, there are no barriers of race (no Greek or Jew); there are no barriers of religious background (circumcised or uncircumcised); there are no barriers of culture (barbarian or Scythian); there are no barriers of social standing (slave or free). Christ destroys the barriers that divide—not destroying our distinctives, but destroying the divisions that may arise from our distinctives.

Maybe the best illustration of this unity that exists in the community of faith comes out of the very history of the letter of the apostle Paul to the Christians at Colossae. It is unlikely that Paul had ever visited Colossae prior to writing this letter. It was probably Epaphras and other converts from Paul's missionary work in Ephesus who began the Colossian church in the mid-50s of the first century.[5]

We learn about a man named Onesimus in Paul's letter to the Colossians and in his letter to Philemon. Onesimus was Philemon's runaway slave who landed in Rome and came to faith under Paul's ministry. Paul encourages Philemon to receive Onesimus "no longer as a slave, but better than a slave, as a dear brother" (Philem. 16).

From the divine perspective, people are people, they are not property and they are not categories. Differences in race and ethnicity, wealth and power, social standing and education—these differences only enrich Christian community that follows the teaching of its founder, Jesus.

Understanding these biblical descriptions and dimensions leads us to conclude that Christian community is intended by Jesus to be a welcoming and safe place—a place where you can be yourself without fear of judgment.

Psychologist and author Larry Crabb has written a book entitled *The Safest Place on Earth.* Crabb suggests that those who see themselves as weary pilgrims are in serious need of connection in community. The size of the community doesn't matter; what matters is that it's "a community of friends who are hungry for God, who know what it means to sense the Spirit moving within them."[6] In this Christian community, believers encourage each other with Scripture and prayer.

We need to be convinced that our small group, our campus club, our spiritual community, our Christian friendship, or our local church is safe if we are going to truly relate like friends and reveal the brokenness of our lives. When Christian friends are authentically welcoming, loving, caring, and embracing—no matter what—then they are creating Christian community that is indeed the safest place on earth.

Theologian and author Lewis Smedes describes a close friend this way: "Someone who knows us better than anyone else does, and yet accepts us, enjoys us, needs us, holds nothing back from us, keeps our secrets, and is there for us."[7]

What should Christian community look like? Paul talks

about a particular style of clothing: "compassion, kindness, humility, gentleness and patience" (Col. 3:12). But these are more than fashionable outfits. They are character qualities and distinctive behaviors of believers that demonstrate to the world what true community can be. The apostle Paul is encouraging the Christian community in Colossae to live like Jesus.

You will notice that the virtues here are all relational virtues—expressed in relationships.[8] As spiritual as you may be, you usually don't exercise these things on a solo road trip or hike in the woods. Compassion, kindness, humility, gentleness, and patience are virtues to be lived out in real-life situations where people meet face to face, heart to heart, life to life. These Christian virtues help Christian community blossom.

TRULY DISTINCTIVE COMMUNITY

It is good and helpful to remind ourselves of the uniqueness and the blessings of living in Christian community. But let's be honest. Living in community is not always what it's cracked up to be—it can be difficult and stressful. You may be familiar with the proverb "familiarity breeds contempt." The longer we observe the shortcomings of people and circumstances around us, the more likely we are to develop attitudes of scorn or cynicism.

There is no gathering of individuals, Christian or otherwise, that exhibits perfect community. Maybe at one time or another we thought there was such a thing as perfection in community—and maybe from a distance, a certain organization or group may have looked perfectly harmonious.

But community can be messy and challenging.

How do we live with all the drama? Above and beyond any formula is the Christian concept of agape love. In the New Living Translation, Colossians 3:14 reads: "Above all, clothe yourselves with love, which binds us all together in perfect harmony."

Francis Schaeffer—a theologian, apologist, and founder of the L'Abri communities—explains that over the centuries Christians have identified themselves in various ways. They have worn lapel pins, necklaces, and even distinctive haircuts to mark themselves as believers. But beyond these superficial identifiers, the one universal and lasting mark of the Christian is a sincere love for one another.[9] Jesus said, "By this everyone will know that you are my disciples, if you love one another" (John 13:35).

But that's not all. Schaeffer goes on to explain the implications of what Jesus taught about Christians loving Christians:

> If I fail in my love toward Christians, it does not prove I am not a Christian. What Jesus is saying, however, is that, if I do not have the love I should have toward all other Christians, the world has the right to make the judgment that I am not a Christian.[10]

That's pretty powerful stuff! So what does it look like to live in authentic Christian relationships? It means, among other things:

- Overlooking the foibles, idiosyncrasies, and thoughtless comments of others
- Forgiving wrong done to you

- Resisting the urge to critique and compete
- Looking for opportunities to cheer people on

Theologian and writer Marva Dawn confesses:

> Those of us who have experienced various kinds of hurts and rejections that make us doubt ourselves *need others* in the Christian community to help us know our worth.[11] (emphasis added)

It's what builds Christian community of any size in any place—authentic love for one another.

REAL ACCOUNTABILITY

Shawn visited my office with an interest in Bible study resources for his small group. But what Shawn received from me that day was nothing near what I received from him. I learned of the amazing dynamics of Shawn's small group. This was a group of six guys who were all committed Christians and who were all committed to each other. Shawn explained how their weekly meetings were a place for true friends to be vulnerable.

A lump formed in my throat as I listened to the depth to which these guys went in being transparent and vulnerable in their Christian walk. A tear came to my eye as I heard the way in which they confessed their sins to each other, shared their struggles, shared their failures, prayed for each other, and read Scripture to each other. I thought to myself, "Wow, these guys are serious disciples of Jesus!"

Shawn told me about one of the guys in his group who

wasn't afraid of getting in Shawn's face if Shawn failed in one of his commitments. This was real accountability in authentic Christian community! The Old Testament text from Ecclesiastes puts it well:

> **Two are better than one,**
> **because they have a good return for their labor:**
> **If either of them falls down,**
> **one can help the other up.**
> **But pity anyone who falls**
> **and has no one to help them up.** (4:9–10)

We are all broken. We are all wounded. We are all weak. We are all needy. Pastor and author John Ortberg talks about this in his book entitled *Everybody's Normal Till You Get to Know Them.* Ortberg puts it this way:

> We all want to look normal, to think of ourselves as normal, but the writers of Scripture insist that no one is "totally normal"—at least not as God defines normal. "*All* we like sheep have gone astray" (Isaiah 53:6 KJV). . . . "*All* have sinned and fall short of the glory of God" (Romans 3:23).[12]

Ortberg says that in Romans 3:23 "the writer of Scripture is trying to establish this deep theological truth: *Everybody's weird.*"[13] Strangely enough, God uses other weird people to bring about our healing and wholeness. God uses broken people to help broken people. And remember—it's God who always shows up in these communities, Christian friendships, and small groups.

John Wesley, known for his Band Societies—accountability

groups where people met in small groups, confessing their sins to one another and praying for one another—said, "Christianity is essentially a social religion; to turn it into a solitary religion is indeed to destroy it."[14]

NEVER WALK ALONE

Offices of public safety on college and university campuses regularly post notices to students to STAY TOGETHER and NEVER WALK ALONE. We might say that this public safety warning is a spiritual life warning as well.

Our God has not created His people to function as lone rangers but are designed as relational beings. Within the body of Christ, God intends for us to live in community— depending upon each other and depending upon our Lord.

So let's determine to establish relationships, to form small groups, to engage in Christ-filled conversation, to journey with godly companions in spiritual community. Let's determine to find safe places where we can come clean and become clean, where we can find grace and give grace with people who care for us as we care for them.

A Step Further

- *Are you able to overlook the shortcomings of others?*

- *Would you consider yourself someone who easily forgives?*

- *Are you able to be a safe person for other Christians in your life?*

- *How is Christian community defined? How is this different from just being a friend to all?*

- *Who is in your Christian community?*

- *Is there anyone you can speak to frankly and openly?*

- *Are you able to receive constructive criticism from a true friend?*

Wouldn't it be great if we
never needed revival, if followers
of Jesus would be faithful in the little
things, living honestly and openly
with others, always longing for God?

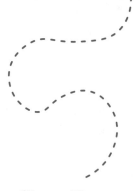

Chapter Nine

Longing for God—Revival

In prioritizing topics for a book on spiritual formation for college students, I sought the advice of student leaders who were respected by their peers. There's one theme that impressed me most because it impressed students most. I worked with a student once who explained it succinctly and memorably. She described her personal spiritual quest as "longing for God." Her desire for intimacy with God was prompted by a need to sense the reality of Jesus' presence in the here and now. In her words, "I have yearned to have that personal friendship with Jesus—like He could sit down next to me in the midst of my struggles."

Throughout my years of college ministry, I have been especially encouraged by spiritually thirsty students desiring to know God more intimately. I've seen it in the passionate singing of worship services. I've seen it in the eyes of young disciples coming forward to receive the elements of the Lord's Supper. I've seen it in my Student Center office as young men and women describe a personal interest in knowing God's will. It's a humbling and deep honor to be on the receiving end of such sensitive issues and personal desires. This is the consistent quality that I have witnessed among those who want to faithfully follow Jesus—they are longing for God.

THE REVIVAL OF 1995

Maybe the most powerful image imprinted on my memory concerning this theme of longing for God is what has become known as "The Revival of 1995." In March of that year, the Wheaton campus experienced a remarkable "visitation of God"—an outpouring of the love of God in a way that influenced hundreds of us individually and all of us corporately.[1]

Wheaton College has had a history of special times of spiritual renewal or awakening that we might call revival. The word "revival" literally means "restoration to life," and that may indeed be the best way to describe what happened at the college over the course of those several days. I've read of similar occurrences at Wheaton in 1936, 1943, 1950, and 1970.[2] (At least one person has suggested a connection between my leaving campus as a student in 1969 and the outbreak of revival in 1970.)

It was on Sunday evening, March 19, 1995, at a World Christian Fellowship (WCF) meeting in Pierce Chapel that something unique and important happened. The WCF program on that evening included testimonies by two students from Howard Payne University in Texas, who described a recent "revival" on their campus. Their presentations were low-key and non-sensational. After each one spoke, the WCF student leader invited anyone else to come forward to speak if they wished; but first, the student leader himself took a few minutes to make a personal confession of his own to the hundreds there for WCF. He openly confessed his sin of pride in his leadership of WCF. He spoke calmly and briefly, but sincerely. The room was quiet.

After a pause, another brave student came forward to a microphone and confessed his own sin of pride. Others came forward; and lines grew on each side of Pierce Chapel. After someone would honestly and vulnerably share a public confession, friends would huddle around and pray over that person while another student began speaking from the other side of the chapel.

What was confessed? There were confessions of pride, hatred, lust, sexual immorality, cheating, dishonesty, materialism, addictions, and self-destructive behavior. There were tears, and there were smiles. There was crying and singing. People confessed their sins to God and to each other, and there was healing. It was biblical. It was orderly. It was sincere. And it honored our Lord.

Time and again, the one who confessed would say something like, "Look. I'm taking off my mask. This is who I am; this is what I have done. I don't want to live like this, but I need your help." Wow. Those were intense moments.

What was happening? If I hadn't witnessed it myself, I wouldn't be able to describe the impact of those hours of student confessions. In their yearning for a closer walk with Jesus, students were confessing their sins to each other, and they embraced each other. The spiritual dynamic of those moments was both horizontal and vertical. Students sought to be obedient to God in confessing to each other, so that they could experience a more intimate fellowship with the Lord.

The meeting that began on Sunday evening went all through the night before finally adjourning on Monday morning at 6 a.m. with students still in line who had waited hours to speak. It was decided that we would conclude for the morning, go on with our academic schedule for the day, and then reconvene at 9:30 that night. Some thought that stopping and starting again would end it all—but it didn't. Pierce Chapel filled to capacity that Monday evening, where a time of worship and confession went from 9:30 p.m. to 2 in the morning. Again, there were still many lined up waiting to speak.

So it was decided that we would meet again on Tuesday night; but this time we had to move the gathering across the street to the sanctuary of a local church because something else had been scheduled in Pierce.[3] Frankly, I was seriously disappointed (actually irate) at our being bumped from Pierce. But God knew that we needed a larger facility. More than thirteen hundred people showed up at the church across the street on Tuesday night, and then more than fifteen hundred people were there on Wednesday night as the last public confession was made at 2 a.m.

The final gathering of the week was on Thursday night in the church sanctuary. Many faculty, staff, and members of the community joined students in dynamic praise and celebration. The church was packed. The worship was electric. People were dancing in the aisles. With so much confession having been done; with so much repentance having been made; with so much reconciliation having been accomplished; there was a sweet, sweet spirit in that place.

The closing moments included an invitation for people who were sensing the call of God to Christian ministry to come forward for a prayer of dedication. Many knelt at the front of the sanctuary to commit themselves to missions and bringing the gospel to the world.

A BIBLICAL FOUNDATION FOR REVIVAL

With this story of revival in mind, let's look at a biblical text written by the apostle Paul to Christians at Ephesus. These words are worth our meditation as we consider the meaning of spiritual renewal and the experience of longing for God.

> So I tell you this, and insist on it in the Lord, that you must no longer live as the Gentiles do, in the futility of their thinking. They are darkened in their understanding and separated from the life of God because of the ignorance that is in them due to the hardening of their hearts. Having lost all sensitivity, they have given themselves over to sensuality so as to indulge in every kind of impurity, and they are full of greed.
>
> That, however, is not the way of life you learned when you heard about Christ and were taught in him in accordance with the truth that is in Jesus. You were taught, with regard to your former way of life, to put off your old self, which is being corrupted by its deceitful desires; to be made new in the attitude of your minds; and to put on the new self, created to be like God in true righteousness and holiness. . . .
>
> Do not let any unwholesome talk come out of your mouths, but only what is helpful for building others

> up according to their needs, that it may benefit those who listen. And do not grieve the Holy Spirit of God, with whom you were sealed for the day of redemption. Get rid of all bitterness, rage and anger, brawling and slander, along with every form of malice. Be kind and compassionate to one another, forgiving each other, just as in Christ God forgave you. (Eph. 4:17–24; 29–32)

In these verses, the apostle is describing what it means to live biblically in Christian community where men and women of faith desire a more intimate fellowship with God. Christian renewal can happen in an individual life, in a small group, on a college campus, or in a local church—but it does not *necessarily* happen in any of these places. Revival happens when Christ followers long to know God better and to obey God more fully—when they "put off the old self" and "put on the new self."

Here's how *The Message* describes this spiritual transition of "putting off" and "putting on":

> Everything—and I do mean everything—connected with that old way of life has to go. It's rotten through and through. Get rid of it! And then take on an entirely new way of life—a God fashioned life, a life renewed from the inside and working itself into your conduct as God accurately reproduces his character in you. (Eph. 4:22–24)

It's possible to misinterpret the significance of the Revival of 1995 by defining it in purely individualistic terms. But as students spoke heart-felt confessions of sin, the members of the congregations on those evenings were more than passive observers, simply watching others who were having personal encounters with God.

Those who weren't actively confessing their own sin were either those who had been sinned against and needed to hear the confession and grant forgiveness—or those able to come alongside the one who was broken—to lift that person up in prayer, to encourage that person, to love that person, and to help keep that person accountable.

The image of the revival that remains in my mind is the image of brokenness and acceptance. Students would spill out the very worst of sins, the most embarrassing of deeds, yet time after time (without exception) the response was grace, acceptance, and love. No judgment. No condemnation. As soon as a confession was completed, people would run to the one who had confessed—six, eight, ten, twelve, or dozens would surround that person. There was embracing and weeping; there was fervent, joyful praying.

What was happening in this spiritual awakening? Men and women, desiring a more intimate fellowship with God, confessed their sins and found the forgiveness of God and the forgiveness of friends.

One of the key words to describe what was happening in those days is "reconciliation." People who were estranged were brought together. There was also gender reconciliation. Guys were confessing sinful attitudes they held against women; and female students confessed how they had reciprocated with similar attitudes that led to hurtful words and actions. There was racial reconciliation. In my memory, none of the campus programs or conferences addressing issues of racial reconciliation over the years have come close to the effectiveness of what happened during that week in March of 1995. In those days, students brokenheartedly confessed their sins of racial insensitivity, prejudice, or even hatred.

As reconciliation happened, barriers came down. Where people had been hurt, there was confession, repentance, and godly sorrow. Love and acceptance began replacing hate and hurt. There was healing. As students sincerely sought to know God better and more fully—they experienced a fresh sense of reconciliation with God and with one another. Students were loving God and singing God's praises, and they were loving one another. They were "building others up" (Eph. 4:29), and they were "forgiving each other" (Eph. 4:32). Nobody was pretending to be perfect. Nobody was boasting of personal accomplishment. All were admitting to be broken sinners seeking the mercy of God—longing for God's presence and grace.

FORGIVENESS ISN'T EASY

The Lord Jesus linked the greatest commandment—to love the Lord your God with all your heart and with all your soul and with all your mind—with the second greatest commandment—to love your neighbor as yourself (Matt. 22:37–39). Here we see how a sincere longing for God naturally leads to a commitment to the difficult but critical practice of forgiveness. Forgiveness that was at the heart of the revival.

What is forgiveness? The word "forgiveness" contains the idea of "letting go" and is used in biblical contexts as "canceling sins."[4] In our text we read, "Be kind and compassionate to one another, forgiving each other, just as in Christ God forgave you" (Eph. 4:32). Here, the apostle challenges us to forgive one another, in the same way that God has forgiven us. That of course, seems impossible—and it is impossible. We are not God. But in some way, our act of forgiving a person can (in at least a small way) reflect God's act of forgiving us.

How does God forgive us? We read the word of the Lord through the prophet in Jeremiah 31:34, "I will forgive their wickedness and will remember their sins no more." When God forgives, God promises that He "will remember our sins no more." Does this mean that God forgets that we have sinned? Not really. God is omniscient, and an omniscient God doesn't forget anything. But God chooses not to remember our sins against us.[5]

We, as human beings, have difficulty remembering things. We are not omniscient; even though we are usually pretty good at remembering the hurtful things people have done. If we are going to choose to imitate God, we will choose not to remember the sins that people have committed against us. To forgive is to promise not to bring those things up (anymore, anytime, anywhere). 1 Corinthians 13:5 puts it this way: "[Love] does not dishonor others, it is not self-seeking, it is not easily angered, it keeps no record of wrongs."

In an earlier era, people would sometimes tie a string around a finger as a memory aid. The string was a reminder not to forget something. When we forgive—we pull off the string and let it go—with no more reminder to remember.

Maybe this sounds too basic. But if it is too basic, then why do we have so much trouble with it? If the Bible is so clear, then why are we so reluctant to forgive those who have offended us, when we know that forgiveness brings healing to the one who gives it as well as the one who receives it?

Henri Nouwen has some perceptive insights here:

> Maybe the reason it seems hard for me to forgive others is that I do not fully believe that I am a forgiven person. If I could fully accept the truth that I am forgiven and do not have to live in guilt or shame, I would really be free. My freedom would allow me to forgive others seventy times seven times. By not forgiving, I chain myself to a desire to get even, thereby losing my freedom. A forgiven person forgives.[6]

We need to remind ourselves of the reality of our own forgiveness. We need to embrace the truth of Scripture: "If we freely admit that we have sinned, we find God utterly reliable and straightforward—he forgives our sins and makes us thoroughly clean from all that is evil" (1 John 1:9 PHILLIPS).

Forgiveness. It's simple, but it isn't easy. Henri Nouwen confesses, "This lifelong struggle lies at the heart of the Christian life."[7] Lewis Smedes understands our weakness and our failure to forgive, yet he cheers us on with these encouraging words:

> If you are *trying* to forgive; even if you manage forgiving in fits and starts, if you forgive today, hate again tomorrow, and have to forgive again the day after, you are a forgiver. Most of us are amateurs, bungling duffers sometimes. So what? In this game nobody is an expert. We are all beginners.[8]

KEEPING SHORT ACCOUNTS WITH GOD

In March of 1998, on the third anniversary of the Wheaton Revival, we had a special chapel remembering the Revival of 1995. Students who were freshmen in 1995 were now seniors in 1998, so it was a good time to reminisce. One of the speakers on that occasion was a former student who had been significantly impacted by the revival and was still living in the area.

On that morning just before chapel, this person approached me to ask if it was all right for him to share a rather unusual thought in his message to students. When I asked what he had in mind, he explained how his grandmother taught him the importance of keeping short accounts with God. He wanted to share this principle of keeping short accounts with God, along with his prayer that Wheaton would never need another revival. An unusual prayer to be sure—but I encouraged him to share it, and he did.

What an incredibly wise word and appropriate message. If we are faithful in seeking an intimate, closer relationship with God, we will keep current our confessions—to God and to one another. Giving this attention to confession allows us to experience the freedom of forgiveness and the joy of reconciliation. And with this level of fellowship, we reduce the need for a giant purging and a great revival.

Don't get me wrong: the Revival of 1995 was a remarkable work of God in the hearts and lives of His people on our campus. Although difficult in many ways, it was also needed. It prepared many for lives of devotion to Christ. Nevertheless, wouldn't it be great if we never needed revival? Wouldn't it be great if followers of Jesus would be faithful in the little things, living honestly and openly with others, always longing for God?

REVIVAL TODAY

It could be that you have found this chapter's description of a campus revival to be historically interesting but personally impractical. Let me urge you to consider the possibility of finding a personal relevance in longing for God and your own "revival."

You may never experience a large-scale revival like the one in this chapter, but that doesn't mean you should be disinterested in finding spiritual renewal through the work of the Holy Spirit in your life.

With the encouragement of Ephesians 4:17–32, we can be challenged to have a new heart for God with a sincere desire to live in obedience to Him. This revival of sorts may indeed happen in the solitude of personal prayer, with a trusted friend, in a small group, or in the life of a church. Revival in our hearts will occur whenever and wherever we seek God's forgiveness for our sin and as we seek the forgiveness of others that we have offended.

This kind of renewal by the Holy Spirit may look different for every person. But if we're serious, the Holy Spirit will work. God is waiting with open arms. Just as God has orchestrated revival in the hearts of people throughout the ages—God can direct revival in your heart as well.

A Step Further

- *Do you honestly long for God? Have you told that to God or anyone else?*

- *When do you feel closest to God?*

- *About how many times have you spoken the phrase (with sincerity), "please forgive me" during this past year?*

- *On a scale of 1–10 (ten being the easiest), how easy is it for you to forgive?*

- *Who comes to mind when you hear the phrase "forgive others"?*

- *In your experience, have you been able to forgive someone who hasn't asked for forgiveness? Maybe the driver who cuts you off? Or the person who mocks you in a social setting? (Use the Bible to support your convictions on this issue.)*

- *What sort of revival have you experienced? Do you long for that? If not, pray and ask God to show you ways in which you could have a closer walk with Him.*

The Scriptures are calling us
to a bold obedience—using the
gifts God has entrusted to
us as His apprentices.

Chapter Ten

Next Steps—Apprenticed to Jesus

At the close of every academic year seniors are barraged by the question, "What are you doing after graduation?" This kind of inquiry is as common today as it has ever been—in fact, it's what I asked myself when I was a student. Although today's student on the verge of graduating doesn't seem to be as clueless as I was, way back when.

As an undergraduate biology major, just completing a liberal arts curriculum, the world was wide-open before me. And I wasn't closing the door to any options. Having thought about medical school for years, I had taken the MCAT. I seriously considered dental school, requiring the DAT. Law school was always a possibility, so I took the LSAT. I completed at least one GRE as a grad school requirement for psychology. It was truly an act of divine intervention that led to my enrollment in a theological seminary that put me on a trajectory leading to pastoral ministry.

Maybe the reason this question about next steps beyond college can be so frustrating is because none of us is able to look into the future with absolute clarity. And, of course, this mystery about what's in store for us around the corner is never ending—no matter what age we may be. Only God knows tomorrow because only God is omniscient, and our Lord has not seen fit to provide us with a blueprint for life. We may wish for a clearer vision of our future, but that may lead us to stumble over the opportunity in front of us at the moment.

APPRENTICES OF JESUS

For those who consider themselves to be Christ followers, it's a no-brainer that one's priority in life should be to follow Jesus. Each next step of our walking should be "in His steps" (1 Pet. 2:21).

I like the word "apprentice," especially when it comes to the spiritual life, and the matter of Christian discipleship. In this final chapter, we will unpack the meaning of apprenticeship as it applies to following Jesus with our lives.

Philosopher and author Dallas Willard is the one who has put me on the track of considering discipleship as apprenticeship to Jesus. In his book, *The Great Omission,* Willard challenges the church to be about the business of making disciples, not just converts. He explains how discipleship is not only for "super Christians." Willard explains, "A disciple is a learner, a student, an apprentice—a practitioner even if only a beginner."[1]

Talmid is the Hebrew word for disciple. In Jesus' day, a *talmid* would submit every aspect of his life to his rabbi. The student's goal was not just to learn what the rabbi knew but to be who the rabbi was. A faithful disciple would follow a teacher so closely that the student would be covered by the dust kicked-up by the sandals of the rabbi.[2]

Our challenge as Christ followers is to be apprentices of Jesus, following as closely as possible to the Rabbi, the master-teacher. Our desire more than anything else is to be like Jesus.[3]

THE PARABLE OF THE TALENTS

So let's stay close to our teacher, Jesus, and hear what He has to say. In His parable of the talents, we learn from our Lord how to be a faithful apprentice. Here we are challenged to use our time well, making the most of every opportunity, exercising our gifts and talents, and (simply put) doing our best to honor God with our life. Matthew 25:14–30 is a lesson in stewardship.

Here, Jesus is preparing his first century disciples for life in His absence. Jesus is on His way to the cross, and His life on earth is about to end—but He is coming again, and at that second advent there will be judgment. So in the meantime, how are we to live as apprentices? The best storyteller who ever lived begins this story by saying:

> **A man going on a journey . . . called his servants and entrusted to them his property. To one he gave five talents, to another two, and to another one, to each according to his ability.** (Matt. 25:14–15 ESV)

To our twenty-first-century ears, this story may sound unusual, but as always, Jesus' stories were historically relevant. In the first century Middle Eastern world, it was common for a wealthy individual to leave town and go on a long journey. Merchants would travel considerable distances to Asia or Europe acquiring goods for a business. With travel unpredictable in those days, who knows how long such a journey would take.[4]

In this story, before departing, the land owner entrusts three servants with a total of eight talents of money. It's hard to tell exactly how much a talent may have amounted to—probably a considerable amount of money. One talent in our story could have been equivalent to about twenty years of a day-laborer's wage.[5] The point that Jesus is making is that the servants are entrusted with the management of significant resources—a big job with big responsibilities for their employer.

Our contemporary understanding of the English word "talent" actually comes from this parable of Jesus.[6] In today's English-speaking world, a talent is a human ability, an individual's capacity to perform or produce. We are quick to recognize talent as special skills using mind or body such as singing or soccer or math.

More pointedly, as disciples of Jesus, we consider our talents to be valuable gifts of God. You and I who wish to be faithful in our stewardship are quick to acknowledge that all of our talents (natural and spiritual) are divine gifts—only on loan to us from God. So if Jesus' story is a parable of the kingdom with Jesus as King, what is Jesus telling us to do?

In this parable we see that each servant received something from the master—something valuable, with important responsibility. But we notice right away that the master distributed different amounts, "each according to his ability" (v. 15). The abilities are God-given; the talents are

God-given—but they are not distributed equally.

That of course, is not news to any of us. We learned a long time ago that individuals are uniquely gifted. People are different. We differ in our natural abilities, our spiritual gifts, our physical strength, our mental capacities, our personalities, our temperaments, and our opportunities. Our personal situations vary greatly. Remember: God distributes abilities and gifts as God sees fit, whatever is best for us—for our good!

It could be that one of your biggest challenges is to understand and accept the fact that we do not all have the same gifts. For many, this reality hits hard and fast when we make the transition from high school to college, or from college and beyond. Suddenly and profoundly, we are struck with the reality that our athletic, musical, intellectual, and relational skills are just not as superior or unique as we may have assumed.

I know for myself, a memorable awakening came in college as I tried to find my way and develop my skill on the football team. Most of my friends don't know that I played football in college. I did. I was a "tailback." Whenever I left the bench and ran out onto the field, the coach would yell at me, "Get your tail back here!"

People are not equally gifted. And coming to grips with that reality may feel brutal as we rub shoulders with talented and creative people. That can be intimidating. We may wonder, "Why is everyone else so capable, and I'm so limited?" Or, "Why does everyone else have so much, and I have so little?" Our Lord gives the gifts, and we need to be okay with that. He's the perfect One—perfectly pure and perfectly good. We can trust our Lord's allotment because

He knows us perfectly, His gifts are perfect, and He does not mess up. We need to see our gifts as God-given, and to use those gifts for God's glory.

The parable continues:

> **He who had received the five talents went at once and traded with them, and he made five talents more. So also he who had the two talents made two talents more. But he who had received the one talent went and dug in the ground and hid his master's money.** (Matt. 25:16–18 ESV)

STEWARDSHIP—WHAT DOES THAT MEAN?

The word "stewardship" is really an archaic word. You don't usually hear that word outside of the church or Christian circles. But I don't know of a better one to describe the management of possessions belonging to someone else. The servants were given talents (belonging to the master) to be used for the good of and the benefit of the master.

The servant with two talents and the servant with five talents both went to work. They worked eagerly and enthusiastically, doing their best for the master. But they are not the stars of this story. Jesus highlights the man with one talent. And why not? It's fair to say that most of us are one-talent people (in a figurative sense). The five-talent person is rare and exceptional.

The one-talent person is tempted to say, "What can I do? With my meager resources, what can be expected of me? Compared to everyone else, I just don't measure up." It's this attitude that got the one-talent man into trouble. How did this servant explain himself? He said in verse 25, "I was afraid." What was he afraid of?

Very likely, he was aware of the larger amounts given to his colleagues, and his fear may have been related to jealousy and envy—evaporating his incentive. Or maybe, with his paltry sum (only twenty years' wages), he couldn't conceive of accomplishing anything significant. More likely, this servant's fear was simply the fear of failure. So he excuses himself and actually places the blame on his master.[7] Look what he says in verse 24:

> **Master . . . I knew that you are a hard man, harvesting where you have not sown and gathering where you have not scattered seed. So I was afraid and went out and hid your gold in the ground.** (Matt. 25:24–25)

There's a fear of failure that can paralyze us. There's a fear of taking risks that can prevent us from stepping out in obedience to our Lord's call to faithful stewardship. Here's how the master responded to the excuse offered by the one-talent servant:

> **You wicked, lazy servant! So you knew that I harvest where I have not sown and gather where I have not scattered seed? Well then, you should have put my money on deposit with the bankers, so that when I returned I would have received it back with interest.** (Matt. 25:26–27)

Or, interestingly, listen to how Eugene Peterson (in *The Message*) paraphrases Jesus' response to the self-justifying servant:

That's a terrible way to live! It's criminal to live cautiously like that! If you knew I was after the best, why did you do less than the least? The least you could have done would have been to invest the sum with the bankers, where at least I would have gotten a little interest.

Did you hear what Jesus said? "It's criminal to live cautiously like that."[8]

One of our regular chapel guests at Wheaton College has been Canon Andrew White, known as "The Vicar of Baghdad," who served for years as pastor of St. George's Anglican Church in Baghdad, Iraq. In a Commencement address, Canon White's message was a surprising one—unexpected to all in attendance. In essence, this was his message: "Don't take care. Take risks." And this is the advice coming from a man who lived and pastored in the heart of Baghdad, in the vicinity of horrific violence—who called followers of Jesus to live out the gospel, risking their lives daily. That's what we do when we are faithful stewards of God's gifts.

Of course, neither Canon White nor the Scriptures are calling us to a reckless foolhardiness, but to a bold obedience—using the gifts God has entrusted to us as His apprentices. In Jesus' parable, the servants demonstrated faithful stewardship by growing their profits with wise investing. We grow the kingdom of God by investing our talents in others, in the local church, in the local community, and in mission work far and wide.

KNOWING AND DOING THE WILL OF GOD

Years ago, I heard the British evangelist John Hunter define the word "success." As soon as I heard this, I wrote it on the inside cover of my Bible: "Success is obedience to the known revealed will of God, regardless of the consequences." This is the teaching of Jesus in the parable of the talents. Our reward—our success—will be revealed at the judgment. And that reward is based on faithful obedience, nothing else!

Maybe you're asking, "But how can I know what God wants me to do? How can I obey God's will if I don't know God's will for my life?" Fair questions. Good questions. It's what we pray for regularly in the Lord's Prayer—"Your will be done" (Matt. 6:10).

Sometimes when we talk about knowing the will of God we think of it in terms of God having a secret plan for our life, and God is hiding that plan behind His back. If our desire is for the will of God—and by that, we mean that we want to know all of the plans and purposes that God has for our life—then we are seeking something that is none of our business. God has never promised us that kind of information. But this is not to say that God doesn't guide us along the way, step by step. God does guide us—by His Word and by His Spirit (2 Tim. 3:16; Gal. 5:16–18).

We see God's promise of guidance in these familiar texts:

> Trust in the Lord with all your heart and lean not on your own understanding; in all your ways submit to him, and he will make your paths straight. (Prov. 3:5–6)

The LORD is my shepherd, I lack nothing.
   He makes me lie down in green pastures,
he leads me beside quiet waters,
   he refreshes my soul.
He guides me along the right paths
   for his name's sake. (Ps. 23:1–3)

One of the first things that comes to my mind when I'm in a decision-making quandry is, "What would Dad do?" In addition to my father's work as a police officer, he was also an attorney. Both of these occupations proved beneficial at times to members of our family. While my father was still living, I could call him at any time for some free legal advice. But since his passing, that resource is unavailable. The One who promised never to leave us or forsake us is readily available to answer the pressing question, "What would our heavenly Father have us do?"

As we know God's Word, we know God's will. Sometimes divine will is pronounced explicitly as in the Ten Commandments (Ex. 20:1–17) or in texts like Micah 6:8, "And what does the LORD require of you? To act justly and to love mercy and to walk humbly with your God." Elsewhere the Scriptures encourage us to discover God's will through the counsel of wise and godly people as in Colossians 3:16, "Let the message of Christ dwell among you richly as you teach and admonish one another with all wisdom."

Scriptures such as Philippians 4:6 describes the importance of prayer, "Do not be anxious about anything, but in every situation, by prayer and petition, with thanksgiving, present your requests to God." In prayer, we ask that God's desires might become our desires. We talk to God in prayer, and we listen to God in prayer. And when it comes to making decisions (even the big decisions concerning vocation, education, location, and relationships), we trust God's Holy Spirit to lead us.

Exactly how does all of this work? While it's tempting to seek fool-proof signs or magic formulas, I think it's simpler than that. It's more about growing in a relationship with our Lord—and walking with God, following close, covered with dust, apprenticed to Jesus.

I find this quote from Dallas Willard helpful in describing what it means to be an apprentice to Jesus: "A disciple is someone whose ultimate goal is to live their life the way Jesus would live it if he were me."[9]

HOW GOD REWARDS

In Jesus' parable—the five-talent servant, the two-talent servant, and the one-talent servant were each given a stewardship. How obedient were they? What was their reward?

The reward is described by Jesus in His parable, beginning at Matthew 25:19, where Jesus says, "After a long time the master of those servants returned and settled accounts with them." In the final analysis, in the last judgment, there is only one thing that matters—there is only one thing that determines our reward as apprentices of Jesus—and that one thing is faithfulness.

The servant given two talents and the servant given five talents were hard-working and ambitious. They doubled their assets; they were successful in their investments, and they were rewarded. But note carefully that the commendation of the master was not based on financial accomplishment. The master said, "Well done, good and faithful servant! You have been faithful" (Matt. 25:21, 23). They were faithful to their master, and that's what determined their reward.

The one-talent servant was not rebuked for failing to show a bottom line profit. It's a fair assumption that this one-talent servant could have been commended by his master even if he had lost part of his holding or all of his holding—if in the process he had made every effort to be faithful.[10]

At the end of the parable, Jesus uses some shocking language, words that freeze us in our tracks.[11] Jesus speaks of "[throwing] that worthless servant outside, into the darkness, where there will be weeping and gnashing of teeth" (Matt. 25:30). Wow. That's a scary thought, and Jesus intends it to be. Yes, there will be a final judgment. Here is a serious warning to those who may only be giving lip-service to repentance and belief in Jesus. It's a warning that God's judgment is serious business.

Up to this point in our consideration of the parable of the talents, the bar has been set high, and we might be wondering if we have the talent and the ability to jump over that bar. Here's the good news: God is for us. God is with us. And we have the promise that God is at work in us.

God always judges His people by their faithfulness—what we do with what we have. In the day of judgment, when our master returns, evaluation will be made on the principle of faithfulness. The number of gifts won't matter. The raw talent and ability won't matter. What will matter is this: Have we been faithful with what we have been given? What counts is what we do with what we have for Christ and His kingdom.

A Step Further

- *What do you think are your greatest strengths?*

- *Think back five, ten, or fifteen years. What talents seem to be consistently there?*

- *Has anyone ever encouraged you by saying that you are good at something? Have you ever told someone they are good at something?*

- *What does it mean to be an apprentice?*

- *Can you be a Christian without being an apprentice of Jesus? Why or why not?*

- *Can you think of someone who you would consider to be a close follower of Jesus? What makes them this way?*

- *What steps could you take today, this month, this year, in using your talents for Christ and His kingdom?*

- *Talk to a close friend sometime this month and exchange "talent" encouragements.*

Notes

Introduction: A Spiritual Walk

1. Helpful discussion on the biblical imagery of "walking" found in Leland Ryken et al., eds., "Walk, Walking," in *Dictionary of Biblical Imagery* (Downers Grove, IL: InterVarsity Press, 1998), 922–23.
2. Leon Morris, *Galatians: Paul's Charter of Christian Freedom* (Downers Grove, IL: InterVarsity Press, 1996), 167.
3. Dallas Willard, *Renovation of the Heart: Putting on the Character of Christ* (Colorado Springs: NavPress, 2002), 22.

Chapter One: The Most Significant Spiritual Challenge in College

1. James Bryan Smith, *Embracing the Love of God* (San Francisco: HarperCollins, 1995), 11.
2. Evelyn Underhill, *An Anthology of the Love of God* (Wilton, CT: Morehouse Barlow, 1976), 15.
3. A. W. Tozer, *The Knowledge of the Holy* (1961; repr., New York: HarperOne, 1978), 98.
4. Dallas Willard, *Renovation of the Heart: Putting on the Character of Christ* (Colorado Springs: NavPress, 2002), 131–32.
5. Warren W. Wiersbe, *The Bible Exposition Commentary,* vol. 2 (Wheaton, IL: Victor Books, 1989), 521.
6. Earl D. Wilson, *Counseling and Guilt* (Dallas: Word Publishing, 1987), 103–04.
7. John R. W. Stott, *Christian Basics: A Handbook of Beginnings, Beliefs and Behaviour* (Grand Rapids, MI: Baker Book House, 1991), 22.
8. Wilson, *Counseling and Guilt,* 96.
9. Ibid.
10. Ibid., 64.
11. Reference to Jerry Kirk's story, "Look at the Birds," is from his chapel message at Wheaton College on Feb. 17, 1994. Rev. Kirk gave permis-

sion for the message to be recorded and archived in the Wheaton College Special Collections, Buswell Library (Audio Chapel Recordings 1955–2009, ID 19940217).

Chapter Two: Weakness—Not Such a Bad Thing

1. Various suggestions concerning the identity of Paul's thorn in the flesh are found in the following: Kenneth L. Chafin, *The Communicator's Commentary: 1, 2 Corinthians* (Waco, TX: Word Books, 1985), 289; F. F. Bruce, *1 and 2 Corinthians* (London: Oliphants, 1971), 248; Philip E. Hughes, *Commentary on the Second Epistle to the Corinthians* (Grand Rapids, MI: Eerdmans, 1962), 444–46; Bruce B. Barton et al., *Life Application Bible Commentary: 1 & 2 Corinthians* (Wheaton, IL: Tyndale House, 1999), 451–52.
2. Gerhard Delling, "skolops," *Theological Dictionary of the New Testament: Vol VII*, ed. G. Friedrich (Grand Rapids, MI: Eerdmans, 1971), 409–10.
3. Paul Tournier, *The Strong and the Weak* (Philadephia: The Westminster Press, 1963), 20–21.
4. N. T. Wright, *Paul for Everyone: 2 Corinthians* (Louisville, KY: Westminster John Knox Press, 2004), 133.
5. Jean Vanier, *Becoming Human* (Toronto: House of Anansi Press Limited, 1998), 93.
6. D. A. Black, "Weakness," in *Dictionary of Paul and His Letters*, ed. Gerald F. Hawthorne, Ralph P. Martin, and Daniel G. Reid (Downers Grove, IL: InterVarsity Press, 1993), 966.

Chapter Three: Perfectionism—Friend or Foe?

1. Harvey Frommer, *The Sports Junkie's Book of Trivia* (Lanham, MD: Taylor Trade Publishing, 2005), 65.
2. Karen Horney, *Neurosis and Human Growth: The Struggle Toward Self-Realization* (New York: W. W. Norton and Company, Inc., 1950), 64–85.
3. Richard Winter, *Perfecting Ourselves to Death: The Pursuit of Excellence and the Perils of Perfectionism* (Downers Grove, IL: InterVarsity Press, 2005).
4. Ibid., 11–12.
5. Ibid., 12–13.
6. Ibid., 33.
7. D. A. Carson, *The Sermon on the Mount: An Evangelical Exposition of Matthew 5–7* (Grand Rapids, MI: Baker Book House, 1978), 54. Also, James Montgomery Boice, *The Sermon on the Mount* (Grand Rapids, MI: Zondervan Publishing House, 1972), 169–75.

8. John R. W. Stott, *Christian Counter-Culture: The Message of the Sermon on the Mount* (Downers Grove, IL: InterVarsity Press, 1978), 121–22. Also, R. V. G. Tasker, *The Gospel According to St. Matthew* (Grand Rapids, MI: William B. Eerdmans Publishing Co., 1961), 70.

9. Stott mentions this in *Christian Counter-Culture*, 122. Also, Tasker in *The Gospel According to St. Matthew*, 70, suggests the same thing and cites C. C. Torrey in *The Four Gospels* (New York: Harper & Brothers, 1947).

10. Thanks to NPR's radio show "Car Talk" for this observation.

11. Dietrich Bonhoeffer, *The Cost of Discipleship* (New York: A Touchstone Book published by Simon & Schuster, 1959), 149.

12. Jeremiah Burroughs, *The Rare Jewel of Christian Contentment* (London: The Banner of Truth Trust, 1964), 41.

13. Ibid., 227–28.

14. *Autarkes* meaning "content" is found only in Phil 4:11; *xortazesthai* from *xortazo* meaning "to be filled or satisfied" is the word used in Phil 4:12. *Autarkeia*, the noun for "contentment" in 1 Tim 6:6 and "having all you need" or "all sufficiency" in 2 Corinthians 9:8.

15. Gordon D. Fee, *Paul's Letter to the Philippians* (Grand Rapids, MI: Eerdmans, 1995), 431–32.

16. Jerry R. Flora, "Searching for an Adequate Life: The Devotional Theology of Thomas R. Kelly," *Spirituality Today* 42, no. 1 (Spring 1990). Historical details of Kelly's life, and the particulars of his story of failure have come from this article by Dr. Flora.

17. Thomas R. Kelly, *A Testament of Devotion* (New York: Harper & Brothers, 1941).

18. Richard M. Kelly, *Thomas Kelly: A Biography* (New York: Harper & Row, 1966), 91f.

19. Kelly, *A Testament of Devotion*, 21.

Chapter Four: Dual Dilemmas—Doubt and Depression

1. Richard Kadison and Theresa Foy DiGeronimo, *College of the Overwhelmed: The Campus Mental Health Crisis and What to Do about It* (San Francisco: Jossey-Bass, 2004).

2. Ibid., 2.

3. Willem A. VanGemeren, "Psalms," in *The Expositor's Bible Commentary*, vol. 5, ed. Frank E. Gaebelein (Grand Rapids, MI: Zondervan Publishing House, 1991), 139.

4. Os Guinness, "I Believe in Doubt," in *Doubt & Assurance*, ed. R. C. Sproul (Grand Rapids, MI: Baker Book House, 1993), 33.

5. James M. Boice, *Psalms 1–41*, vol. 1 (Grand Rapids, MI: Baker Books, 1994), 106.

6. H. C. Leupold, *Exposition of the Psalms* (Grand Rapids, MI: Baker Book House, 1969), 135.

7. Peter C. Craigie, *Word Biblical Commentary: Psalms 1–50*, vol. 19 (Waco, TX: Word Books, 1983), 142–43.

8. Sinclair B. Ferguson, *Deserted by God?* (Grand Rapids, MI: Baker Books, 1993), 25.

9. Cornelius Plantinga Jr., *Beyond Doubt: Faith-Building Devotions on Questions Christians Ask* (Grand Rapids, MI: Eerdmans Publishing Co., 2002), 37.

10. Ulrich Luz is quoted by Frederick Dale Bruner in *Matthew: A Commentary—Volume 2: The Churchbook, Matthew 13–28, Revised and Expanded Edition* (Grand Rapids, MI: William B. Eerdmans Publishing Co., 1990), 78.

11. Paul Tournier, *To Resist or To Surrender?* (Louisville, KY: Westminster John Knox Press, 1964), 47.

12. Paul Tournier, *The Person Reborn* (London: SCM, 1967), 106.

13. Plantinga, *Beyond Doubt*, 37.

Chapter Five: An Unclaimed Gift—the Sabbath

1. James Surowiecki offers an insightful commentary on the concept of "overwork" in "The Cult of Overwork," in the Financial Page of *The New Yorker* (January 27, 2014). In this article, Surowiecki says, "Overwork has become a credential of prosperity."

2. John Ortberg, *The Life You've Always Wanted* (Grand Rapids, MI: Zondervan Publishing House, 1997), 81–82.

3. R. Laird Harris, ed., *Theological Wordbook of the Old Testament*, vol. 2 (Chicago: Moody Press, 1980), 902.

4. Walter A. Elwell, ed., "Sabbath," *Baker Encyclopedia of the Bible*, vol. 2, J–Z (Grand Rapids, MI: Baker Book House, 1988), 1877.

5. Terry Hershey, *The Power of Pause: Becoming More by Doing Less* (Chicago: Loyola Press, 2009), 142–45.

6. In my Wheaton College chapel message of Nov. 22, 1996, I included the statement: "Lee gave me permission to tell this story."

7. Bob Thune, "Becoming What We Behold," *Tabletalk* 42, no. 8 (August 2018), 64–65.

Chapter Six: Sexuality and Singleness

1. Saint Augustine, *Confessions: A New Translation by Sarah Ruden* (New York: The Modern Library, 2017), 3.

2. Lisa Graham McMinn, *Sexuality and Holy Longing: Embracing Intimacy in a Broken World* (San Francisco, CA: Jossey-Bass, 2004), 76.

3. Craig S. Keener, *The IVP Bible Background Commentary: New Testament* (Downers Grove, IL: InterVarsity Press, 1993), 96. Keener identifies the

two leading rabbinic schools in Jesus day as the Hillel school and the Shammai school who debated the grounds for divorce implied in Deuteronomy 24:1–4. Keener writes: "The school of Shammai, predominant in Jesus' day, argued that the passage allowed divorce only if one's spouse was unfaithful; the school of Hillel, which eventually won out, said that a man could divorce his wife if she burned the toast."

4. Malachi 2:14 identifies marriage as a "covenant" relationship.

5. Timothy Keller, *The Meaning of Marriage: Facing the Complexities of Commitment with the Wisdom of God* (New York: Dutton, 2011), 224.

6. According to US Census Bureau statistics for estimated median age at first marriage by sex for 2018 found at www.census.gov/data/tables/time-series/demo/families/marital.html.

7. Rebecca Wind, "Premarital Sex Is Nearly Universal among Americans, and Has Been for Decades," Guttmacher Institute Media Center, December 19, 2006, www.guttmacher.org/media/nr/2006/12/19/index .html. The study was done by the National Survey of Family Growth, and the report was published by Lawrence Finer in the January/February 2006 issue of *Public Health Reports.*

8. Kate Julian, "The Sex Recession," *The Atlantic,* December 2018, 78–94.

9. Lauren F. Winner, *Real Sex: The Naked Truth about Chastity* (Grand Rapids, MI: Baker Publishing Group, 2005), 29–30.

10. Craig Blomberg, *NIV Application Commentary: 1 Corinthians* (Grand Rapids, MI: Zondervan Publishing House, 1994), 126–27.

11. Winner, *Real Sex,* 38.

12. Craig S. Keener, *Matthew* (Downers Grove, IL: InterVarsity Press, 1997), 299.

13. D. A. Carson, "Matthew," in *The Expositor's Bible Commentary,* vol. 8 (Grand Rapids, MI: Zondervan Publishing House, 1984), 419.

14. Keller in *The Meaning of Marriage,* p. 194, cites Stanley Hauerwas, *A Community of Character* (South Bend, IN: University of Notre Dame Press, 1991), 174.

15. I'm indebted to Rosaria Butterfield for her reference to John Piper's sermon in *Openness Unhindered: Further Thoughts of an Unlikely Convert on Sexual Identity and Union with Christ* (Pittsburgh: Crown and Covenant Publications, 2015), 129. Piper's sermon of April 29, 2007, can be located at: www.desiringgod.org/sermons/single-in-christ-a-name-better-than-sons-and-daughters.

16. Specific biblical texts bearing on the issue of homosexuality are: Genesis 19:1–8; Judges 19:16–25; Leviticus 18:22; 20:13; Deuteronomy 23:18; Romans 1:26–27; 1 Corinthians 6:9–10; 1 Timothy 1:10; and Jude 7.

17. For a thorough study of biblical texts related to homosexuality see Robert A. J. Gagnon, *The Bible and Homosexual Practice: Texts and Hermeneutics* (Nashville: Abingdon Press, 2001).

18. Wesley Hill, *Washed and Waiting: Reflections on Christian Faithfulness & Homosexuality* (Grand Rapids, MI: Zondervan, 2016).

19. Butterfield, *Openness Unhindered*, 6.

20. Ibid., 6.

Chapter Seven: Beyond Me-ism—Servanthood

1. Craig S. Keener, *The IVP Bible Background Commentary: New Testament* (Downers Grove, IL: InterVarsity Press, 1993), 217. For cultural perspectives see also Darrell L. Bock, *Luke* (Downers Grove, IL: InterVarsity Press, 1994), 197.

2. William Barclay, *The Gospel of Luke* (Philadelphia: The Westminster Press, 1953), 141. Barclay explains: "In the fifth century Jerome tells us that it was still called 'The Red, or Bloody Way.'"

3. Leon Morris, *The Gospel According to St. Luke* (Grand Rapids, MI: William B. Eerdmans Publishing Co., 1974), 189.

4. A number of commentators have observed the reluctance of the lawyer to pronounce the word "Samaritan," including James M. Boice, *The Parables of Jesus* (Chicago: Moody, 1983), 153.

5. Bruce B. Barton, Dave Veerman, and Linda K. Taylor, *Life Application Bible Commentary: Luke* (Wheaton, IL: Tyndale House Publishers, Inc., 1997), 282.

6. The author who encouraged me most to pursue the notion that the lawyer was seeking only "the least he could do" is John Claypool, *Stories Jesus Still Tells: The Parables* (New York: McCracken Press, 1993), 102.

7. Stuart Briscoe describes the meaning of "neighbor" clearly and succinctly in *Patterns for Power: Parables of Luke* (Glendale, CA: Regal Books, 1979), 44.

8. For identifying the concept of "universal neighborhood" in the parable of the Good Samaritan, I am indebted to R. C. Sproul, *The Parables of Jesus,* DVD series, disc 2 of 2; no. 9, "Parable of the Good Samaritan" (Orlando, FL: Ligonier Ministries, 2012).

9. David E. Garland, *Zondervan Exegetical Commentary on the New Testament: Luke* (Grand Rapids, MI: Zondervan, 2011), 448.

10. Martin Luther King Jr., *Strength to Love* (New York: Harper & Row, 1963), 37–38.

11. Simon Kistemaker extends the application of Jesus' parable beyond the individual to the national in *The Parables of Jesus* (Grand Rapids, MI: Baker Book House, 1980), 174.

12. Donald P. McNeill, Douglas A. Morrison, and Henri J. M. Nouwen, *Compassion: A Reflection on the Christian Life* (New York: Doubleday, 1982), 4.

13. Ibid.

14. Source materials here attributed to Siang-Yang Tan are from his co-authored book: Siang-Yang Tan and Douglas H. Gregg, *Disciplines of the Holy Spirit: How to Connect to the Spirit's Power and Presence* (Grand Rapids, MI: Zondervan Publishing House, 1997), 200.
15. Ibid.
16. Richard J. Foster, *Celebration of Discipline: The Path to Spiritual Growth* (New York: Harper & Row, 1978), 122.

Chapter Eight: Living in a Safe Place—Community

1. Frank Bruni, "The Real Campus Scourge," *New York Times,* September 2, 2017, https://www.nytimes.com/2017/09/02. In 2016 the American College Health Association surveyed about twenty-eight thousand students on fifty-one campuses where 60 percent said that they had "felt very lonely" in the previous twelve months.
2. C. S. Lewis, *The Four Loves* (New York: Harcourt Brace Jovanovich, 1960), 96–97.
3. This definition of community is originally presented in: Thomas H. Naylor, William H. Willimon, and Magdalena R. Naylor, *The Search for Meaning* (Nashville: Abingdon, 1994), 128. It is quoted in: William H. Willimon and Thomas H. Naylor, *The Abandoned Generation: Re thinking Higher Education* (Grand Rapids, MI: William B. Eerdmans Publishing Co., 1995), 145.
4. Dietrich Bonhoeffer, *Life Together* (New York: Harper & Brothers, 1954), 21.
5. A concise yet excellent source of historical background material is provided by Peter T. O'Brien, "Colossians," in *New Bible Commentary*, ed. G. J. Wenham, J. A. Motyer, D. A. Carson, R. T. France (Downers Grove, IL: InterVarsity Press, 1994), 1260–62.
6. Larry Crabb, *The Safest Place on Earth: Where People Connect and Are Forever Changed* (Nashville: W Publishing Group, 1999), 19.
7. Lewis B. Smedes, *Caring & Commitment: Learning to Live the Love We Promise* (San Francisco: Harper & Row, 1988), 46.
8. Concerning this concept of relational virtues, I am indebted to William Barclay, *The Letters to the Philippians, Colossians, and Thessalonians* (Philadelphia: The Westminster Press, 1959), 188.
9. Francis A. Schaeffer, *The Church at the End of the 20th Century* (Downers Grove, IL: InterVarsity Press, 1970), 133.
10. Ibid., 137. In this chapter, "The Mark of the Christian," Schaeffer makes a distinction between "loving neighbors" and "loving fellow believers." He writes: "*All* men are our neighbors, and we are to love them as ourselves. . . . This is, of course, the whole point of Jesus' story of the good Samaritan. . . . So when Jesus gives the special command to love our

Christian brothers, it does not negate the other command. . . . The two commands reinforce each other" (134).

11. Marva Dawn, *Truly the Community: Romans 12 and How to Be the Church* (Grand Rapids, MI: Eerdmans Publishing Co., 1992), 172.

12. John Ortberg, *Everybody's Normal Till You Get to Know Them* (Grand Rapids, MI: Zondervan Publishing, 2003), 15.

13. Ibid., 16.

14. J. Wesley Bready, *England: Before and After Wesley: The Evangelical Revival and Social Reform* (New York: Harper & Brothers, 1938), 202.

Chapter Nine: Longing for God—Revival

1. During the following summer following the Revival of 1995, two college faculty members chronicled the event with a book: Timothy Beougher and Lyle Dorsett, eds., *Accounts of a Campus Revival: Wheaton College 1995* (Wheaton, IL: Harold Shaw Publishers, 1995).

2. Mary Dorsett, *Revival at Wheaton* (Wheaton, IL: International Awakening Press, 1994).

3. The College Church in Wheaton (a congregation independent of Wheaton College) graciously provided the use of their sanctuary for our meetings.

4. Greek: *aphesis*, is translated *forgiveness* in English and has the meaning of "sending away" or "letting go." See also Everett F. Harrison, ed., *Baker's Dictionary of Theology* (Grand Rapids, MI: Baker Book House, 1960), 226.

5. Jay E. Adams, *From Forgiven to Forgiving* (Wheaton, IL: Victor Books, 1989), 17–18.

6. Henri J. M. Nouwen, *Show Me the Way* (New York: The Crossroad Publishing Co., 1992), 44.

7. Ibid.

8. Lewis B. Smedes, *Forgive and Forget: Healing the Hurts We Don't Deserve* (San Francisco: Harper & Row, 1984), 151.

Chapter Ten: Next Steps—Apprenticed to Jesus

1. Dallas Willard, *The Great Omission: Reclaiming Jesus's Essential Teachings on Discipleship* (New York: HarperCollins, 2006), xi.

2. Ray Vander Laan, "In the Dust of the Rabbi: Learning to Live as Jesus Lived," September 8, 2015, DVD.

3. Willard, *The Great Omission*, 7.

4. John Claypool, *Stories Jesus Still Tells: The Parables* (New York: Mc-Cracken Press, 1993), 41.

5. Klyne R. Snodgrass, *Stories with Intent: A Comprehensive Guide to the Parables of Jesus* (Grand Rapids, MI: William B. Eerdmans Publishing Co., 2008), 528.

6. Ibid.
7. Claypool, *Stories Jesus Still Tells*, 50–52.
8. I was directed to this paraphrase by Luci Shaw in, *The Crime of Living Cautiously: Hearing God's Call to Adventure* (Downers Grove, IL: Inter-Varsity Press, 2005), 20–21.
9. John Ortberg, *Eternity Is Now in Session: A Radical Rediscovery of What Jesus Really Taught about Salvation, Eternity, and Getting to the Good Place* (Carol Stream, IL: Tyndale House Publishers, 2018), 60.
10. Daniel R. Seagren, *The Parables* (Wheaton, IL: Tyndale House Publishers, 1978), 34.
11. Snodgrass, *Stories with Intent*, 536.

EVERY TWENTYSOMETHING NEEDS A LITTLE BLACK BOOK OF SECRETS.

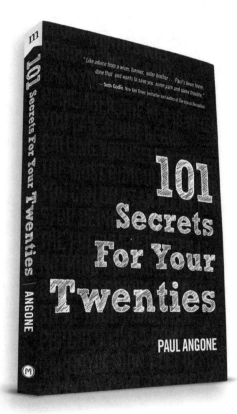

MOODY
Publishers®

From the Word to Life®

After a decade-long search, Paul Angone has compiled 101 secrets especially for twentysomethings—secrets concerning work, relationships, and faith. This humorous book will help equip twentysomethings to live with confidence and wisdom in their post-college years.

978-0-8024-1084-9 | also available as an eBook

ADULTING GOT YOU DOWN?

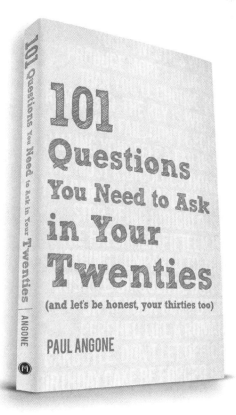

A STUDY ON SEX THAT GOES BEYOND "JUST DON'T DO IT."

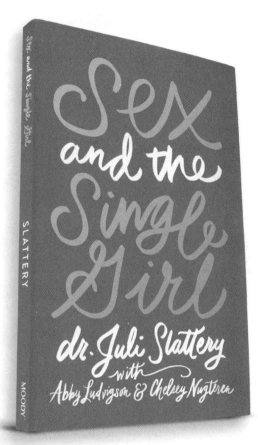

HOW TO MAKE THE MOST OF YOUR 20s

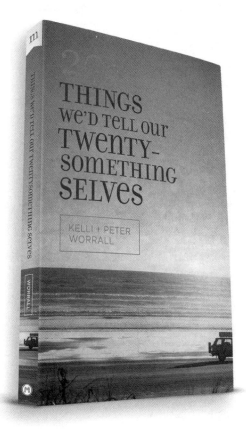

In *20 Things We'd Tell Our Twentysomething Selves*, professors Peter and Kelli Worrall look back on their twenties to give you the best of what they've learned. With humility, warmth, and brilliant storytelling they invite you not only into their wisdom, but into their very lives, helping you make your twenties count.

978-0-8024-1334-5 | also available as an eBook

HOW TO MAKE THE MOST OF YOUR